S. W. Crittenden

Sacraments of the Church

S. W. Crittenden

Sacraments of the Church

ISBN/EAN: 9783337260637

Printed in Europe, USA, Canada, Australia, Japan

Cover: Foto ©Lupo / pixelio.de

More available books at **www.hansebooks.com**

SACRAMENTS

OF

THE CHURCH.

BY

Rev. S. W. CRITTENDEN.

PHILADELPHIA:
PRESBYTERIAN PUBLICATION COMMITTEE,
1334 CHESTNUT STREET.
NEW YORK: A. D. F. RANDOLPH, 770 BROADWAY.

Entered according to Act of Congress, in the year 1869, by
WM. L. HILDEBURN, TREASURER,
in trust for the
PRESBYTERIAN PUBLICATION COMMITTEE,
In the Clerk's Office of the District Court of the United States, for the Eastern District of Pennsylvania.

WESTCOTT & THOMSON,
Stereotypers, Philada.

Rev. Samuel W. Crittenden,

    Dear Sir :—

        The subscribers, members of the Walnut Street Presbyterian Congregation of this city, having heard, from the pulpit of our church, your series of sermons, four in number, on the Sacraments, would be pleased to obtain your consent to their publication.

Having been instructed and profited by their contents, we would be glad to see them in print, that others may be benefited as we have been, and that their usefulness may be extended by their publication.

      Very Truly,

        Your Friends,

Joseph Allison,	D. Steinmetz,
G. H. Christian,	J. G. Fine,
Jno. Power,	H. A. Rood,
Samuel Field,	A. L. Massey,
Wm. Moland,	H. M. Lewis,
E. McHenry,	Edward Miller.

Philadelphia, *September*, 1868.

PHILADELPHIA, *October* 1, 1868.

To Hon. Judge Allison,

    Messrs. Christian, Power, Field and Others,

        Dear Brethren :—

Your very kind and complimentary request, for my consent to the publication of a series of sermons delivered by me on the Sacraments, has been received.

These sermons were not written with a view to publication, and I do not deem them exhaustive of the subject, nor worthy of the flattering notice they have received. Yet, if they have met a felt want with you, they may, with God's blessing, do as much for others.

Yielding, therefore, to your judgment rather than to my own, I cheerfully accede to your request. But, in so doing, will ask your permission to do away with the sermon style, to rearrange somewhat the order of treatment of the different topics, and to make such other modifications as shall present the subject-matter of these discourses in a form better suited for general reading, and especially *more convenient as a manual of reference* on the subject of the Sacraments.

    With sincere regard,

        Yours in the Gospel of Christ,

            S. W. Crittenden.

CONTENTS.

CHAPTER I.

INTRODUCTION.

PAGE

Origin and meaning of the word "Sacrament."—Its use in Ecclesiastical Latin.—Its signification in the Vulgate.—Its more restricted Theological sense.—Augustine's definition of Church Sacraments—why erroneous. 11

Number of sacraments multiply as the Church becomes corrupt.—Number declared to be seven by Council of Florence, A. D. 1438.—Only two of these admitted by Protestants to be properly sacraments.—Definition of a Church Sacrament, as given in our Shorter Catechism.. 14

Papal doctrine in regard to the efficacy of the sacraments.—Canons of the Council of Trent, A. D. 1547.—Other Roman Catholic authorities.—Luther's view of the efficacy of the sacraments.—The Reformed doctrine on the subject, as held by nearly all Protestants.. 17

CHAPTER II.

DESIGN, EFFICACY AND MODE OF BAPTISM.

Baptism of Jewish proselytes prior to the Christian era—an unauthorized, yet significant appendage to Circumcision.—General expectation in the Jewish mind that both Christ and his forerunner would baptize.—Examination of the time when Christian baptism commenced.—John's baptism not Christian baptism.—His baptism, like himself, belonged to the old dispensation.—The baptism performed by Christ's disciples prior to the resurrection not Christian baptism.—Baptism of three thousand on the day of Pentecost, the first Christian baptism.................... 30

The *design* of baptism.—It is a symbol of purification, and suggests needed inward cleansing by the Holy Spirit.—Immersion theory not tenable.............. 44

The *efficacy* of baptism.—God's signet to attest his promise.—Promise sure where all the conditions are fulfilled... 57

The *mode* of Christian baptism.—Sprinkling, pouring and immersion, each valid.—The last the least significant and appropriate of the three modes.—No proof that immersion was ever practiced in the apostolic Church—on the contrary, much to show that baptism was usually, if not always, by either pouring or sprinkling.—Arguments against immersion as the exclusive mode.. 61

CHAPTER III.

THE PROPER SUBJECTS OF BAPTISM.

Baptism first—complete Indoctrination afterward.—Adults to confess Christ and be baptized as soon as they believe.—Infant children of believers also to receive baptism.—Such baptized children, church members.—Our Standards teach this.—The Bible sanctions it.—Question as to female Infants.—Christ's commission to baptize intended to include Infants.—The Apostles so understood it, and accordingly baptized whole households........................ 83

Objections against Infant baptism considered and answered:—1. That the argument from circumcision is good for nothing, because that ceremony was a national rite, and not a Church ordinance :—2. That faith is requisite to a membership in Christ's Church; that Infants cannot exercise faith, and therefore cannot properly be admitted to the Church :—3. That all Church members have a right to partake of both its sacraments; and that consistency would require us, who recognize Infants as members, to bring them with us to the sacrament of the Lord's Supper :—4. That it is unjust to place the seal of church-membership upon an unconscious Infant; and to make solemn vows for that infant, binding him to their fulfillment :—5. That the tendency of such teaching and such practice as we adopt in regard to Infants is to lower the standard of personal piety in the Church... 105

Evils springing from the failure of the Church to comprehend and act on the true doctrine :—1. Many conversions prevented, which might have taken place in early infancy :—2. The spiritual treatment of baptized children after they arrive at years of discretion, oftentimes unwise and pernicious...................... 123

CHAPTER IV.

SACRAMENT OF THE LORD'S SUPPER.

The *design* of this Sacrament.—A new memorial rite for the Church.—A memorial of Christ.—More specifically, of his death............................. 129

Early Church practices in relation to the Lord's Supper, and *historical development* of *doctrinal errors* concerning it.—Daily celebration of the ordinance in the apostolic Church.—At first an appendage to the Love Feast.—Hence many abuses.—Love Feasts forbidden in churches by Council of Carthage, A. D. 397.—Undue exaltation of the material elements.—Consecrated Bread used as an amulet.—Withholding of the cup from the laity.—Elevation of the bread and wine before distribution.—Real presence of Christ in the symbols asserted.—Transubstantiation—declared by Radbert, A. D. 831—decreed by Pope Innocent III., A. D. 1215.—Adoration of the "Host."—Masses for the dead... 141

Scriptural refutation of these errors..................... 159

Who are *proper participants* of this ordinance?—The *effect* of partaking—upon those who partake unworthily—upon worthy participants................ 166

Introduction.

"Search the Scriptures; for in them ye think ye have eternal life: and they are they which testify of me."—JOHN v. 39.

"These were more noble than those in Thessalonica, in that they received the word with all readiness of mind, and searched the Scriptures daily, whether those things were so."—ACTS xvii. 11.

"All Scripture is given by inspiration of God, and is profitable for doctrine, for reproof, for correction, for instruction in righteousness: that the man of God may be perfect, thoroughly furnished unto all good works."—2 TIM. iii. 16, 17.

"Prove all things; hold fast that which is good."—1 THESS. v. 21.

CHAPTER I.

Introduction.

ORIGIN and meaning of the word "Sacrament."—Its use in Ecclesiastical Latin.—Its signification in the Vulgate.—Its more restricted Theological sense.—Augustine's definition of Church Sacraments—why defective.

Number of sacraments multiply as the Church becomes corrupt.—Number declared to be seven by Council of Florence, A. D. 1438.—Only two of these admitted by Protestants to be properly sacraments.—Definition of a Church Sacrament, as given in our Shorter Catechism.

Papal doctrine in regard to the efficacy of the sacraments.—Canons of the Council of Trent, A. D. 1547.—Other Roman Catholic authorities.—Luther's view of the efficacy of the sacraments.—The Reformed doctrine on the subject, as held by nearly all Protestants.

THE term "Sacrament" is of Latin origin. The Latin verb *sacrare* means to set apart as sacred, to consecrate. From this is formed the noun *sacramentum*, which, in its original use, denoted the sum that the Roman law required to be deposited by each of the two parties to a suit—so called because the deposit was made in a sacred place, or because the sum deposited by the losing party was used for religious purposes. Subsequently it was applied to the oath of allegiance taken by the Roman soldier, by which he consecrated himself entirely to the service of the emperor, solemnly promising to remain faithful to him under all vicissitudes.

In ecclesiastical Latin the use of the word *sacramentum* was at first very general.

Thus the sign of the cross, anointing with oil, and in short any significant sacred rite was called a sacrament. It was also used by the Roman Church to denote the whole gospel, as by the Greeks the gospel was called a *mystery*.

In the sense of a sacred thing, or a mystery, it found a place in the Vulgate, or common Latin translation of the Bible, in which the Greek word signifying a mystery (μυστήριον) was rendered *sacramentum*. Thus in Paul's first Epistle to Timothy, 3d chapter and 16th verse, rendered in our version, "Without controversy great is the *mystery* of godliness," the reading in the Vulgate is, "Manifestly great is the *sacrament* of piety." [See also Eph. iii. 3 and i. 9.]

In a more restricted theological sense, the word came to be used for a divinely instituted rite, in which, under some outward form, the promise to confer an inward spiritual gift was signified and sealed. Hence it was applied to baptism and the Lord's Supper; and these ordinances which the Greeks had called mysteries (μυστήρια), as indicating that there was a depth of hidden spiritual meaning wrapped up in the outward signs used in their administration, were in the Roman Church denominated sacraments (*sacramenta*).

It became necessary, therefore, for the Roman theologians to give a specific, theological definition to the word in its new and restricted use. Accordingly we find that "Augustine describes the sacraments as being *visible signs representing invisible divine things*, by means of which the divine matter is exhibited, as it were, by writing, by outward language."* This definition was too general, as under it might be included many symbolic signs, which nevertheless are wanting in some essentials that pertain to baptism and the Lord's Supper. And perhaps it was partly owing to this imperfect conception of the "sacrament, as a holy symbol," that Augustine, with his contemporaries, was led to call other rites by that name, and to admit that there were *four* sacraments.†

In the later and more corrupt age of the Church, the disposition to multiply her sacraments perpetually increased, until, in A. D. 1124, Bishop Otto of Bamberg is said to have instructed those whom he was about to baptize that there were "*seven*

* Neander's Ch. Hist., vol ii. p. 662.   † Same, p. 664.

sacraments," and that "by these were designated the gifts of the Holy Ghost, which were the appointed means of upholding and strengthening the faithful."* This is worthy of notice as being the first historical mention† of what afterward became the settled doctrine of the Papal Church. Other scholastics of the Middle Ages contended for as many as *ten* or *twelve* sacraments. But the number was at last definitely settled by the Council of Florence, A. D. 1438, as *seven;* and the Council of Trent, in the sixteenth century, pronounced the usual anathema against all who made the number greater or less.‡ These seven were baptism, the eucharist or Lord's Supper, confirmation, penance, extreme unction, orders and matrimony: all of which are still accounted as sacraments in the Church of Rome. But Protestants deny that any

* Nean. Ch. Hist., vol. iv. p. 8.
† Same, p. 335.
‡ Council of Trent, Sess. 7, Can. 1.

of them are sacraments except the first two, baptism and the Lord's Supper.

Many definitions have been framed with a view to exclude from the name of sacrament every rite which has been, or may be, falsely so called. Of all these definitions, perhaps none is better than that which is given in answer to the 92d question in our Shorter Catechism:—"A sacrament is a holy ordinance instituted by Christ; wherein, by sensible signs, Christ and the benefits of the new covenant are represented, sealed and applied to believers." By this definition three things are made essential to a sacrament:—

1. That it be an ordinance *instituted by Christ*.

2. That it *employ sensible signs*, i. e., signs manifest to the senses.

3. That it be appointed to *represent, seal* and *apply* Christ and the benefits of the new covenant.

But confirmation, penance, extreme unction, orders and matrimony, all fail in some of these essentials, and are not therefore to be regarded as sacraments. Baptism and the Lord's Supper, however, fulfill all the conditions of the definition. They are ordinances instituted by Christ. In their administration sensible signs are employed. And they are designed to represent, seal and apply to the believer Christ and the benefits of the new covenant. All Protestants agree, therefore, in calling these two ordinances sacraments, and in asserting that the name cannot correctly be applied to any other church rite, or symbol, or practice.

But, besides the errors which thus crept into the Papal Church as to the true import of the term sacrament, and as to the number of the sacraments, a theory of a much more pernicious character sprang up by degrees, and was at length put forth as an authoritative dogma. This theory is, that there is an inherent power in the sacraments themselves, so that when properly administered, and unless positively resisted by those to whom administered, they certainly convey the grace of which they are the signs.*

* The *Council of Trent* [A. D. 1547] decreed this error as follows: "If any one saith, that the sacraments of the new law do not *contain* the grace which they signify; or, that they do not *confer* that grace on those who do not place an obstacle thereunto; as though they were merely outward signs of grace or justice received through faith, and certain marks of the Christian profession, whereby believers are distinguished amongst men from unbelievers; let him be anathema."—*Sacram. Can.* vi.

"If any one saith, that by the said sacraments of the new law grace is not conferred through the act performed [*ex opere operato*], but that faith alone in the divine promise suffices for the obtaining of grace; let him be anathema."—*Sacram. Can.* viii.

Bellarmine, one of the most reliable Roman Catholic authorities, thus states this papistical doctrine: "That which actively and directly and instrumentally accomplishes [*efficit*] the grace of justification is that external act alone [*sola actio illa externa*] which is called a sacrament, and this is termed the *opus operatum*, to be received *passively*, that so this same (external act) may be a sacrament to confer grace by the act done (*ex opere operato*), that is, to confer grace by the

The right administration of the ordinance, however, is everything. The officiator must be a priest, properly ordained, and must have the *right intention;* that is, he must at the time he goes through the service invariably *will* that the sacrament produce its legitimate effect in order to make it efficacious.* This virtually places the Church and all the blessings signified by her ordinances at the mere will and caprice of the officiating priest—a doctrine too monstrous and absurd to be for one moment tolerated.

But, according to this theory, if the qualifications and intention of the officiator be right, the grace is certainly imparted, whether the recipient has any positive faith

power of the sacramental action itself, instituted by God for this purpose, not on account of the merit of the agent or recipient."—*De Sacram.* ij. 1.

* "If any one saith, that, in ministers, when they effect and confer the sacraments, there is not required *the intention* at least *of doing what the Church does;* let him be anathema."—*Coun. Trent, Sacram. Can.* xi.

or not: only, he must not be in a state of positive resistance. A negative, and not a positive, attitude is all that is required of him. If he will passively receive the sacrament, he will therewith receive the virtue which inheres in it. Just as a man who is sick, if he will consent to take a medicine suited to his disease, may be cured, whether he believes in the efficacy of the medicine or not; so the recipient of the sacrament will be a partaker of its full benefit, even though he have no active or positive faith.*

---

* *Rt. Rev. Bishop Hay*, in his "Sincere Christian Instructed," chap. xix., says, "There is a very homely, but clear example which explains it exactly: namely, that of writing upon paper. In order to write there is required a pen full of ink, a hand to apply it to the paper, and paper to receive it. Now, when the pen full of ink is applied to the paper by a proper hand, and there is no impediment on the paper itself, the writing never fails to be performed; but if the paper should be oiled, and by that means rendered indisposed for the receiving the ink, though the pen be full of ink, and applied by the most skillful hand to the paper, yet one single letter will not be formed by it; not from any failure on the part of the pen, or of the hand applying it, but be-

This totally destroys the doctrine of salvation by faith, and substitutes in its place the saving virtue of priestly manipulations.

Luther attempted to uproot this error, but

cause the paper itself is perfectly incapable of receiving the ink upon it. Now, the sacraments are like the pen full of ink, for, being ordained by Jesus Christ as the sacred canals through which his divine grace flows from his blessed wounds to our souls, they contain that grace in great abunddance ; the person who administers the sacrament is like the hand who applies the pen to the paper, and the soul of the receiver is like the paper itself. If then this paper be in a proper state, that is, if the soul be well disposed, these heavenly canals will never fail to communicate to her such a portion of the grace they contain as she is capable of receiving ; but, if the paper be oiled, if the soul be indisposed and incapable of receiving the grace, then the grace cannot be bestowed, because the soul cannot receive it."

Bishop Hay lived in England, and would naturally endeavor to make the doctrines of the Papal Church as little offensive as he could in a Protestant community. Hence his illustration, although in fact containing the same fatal error of considering the grace to lie in the sacraments themselves, and to be communicated by them, without any active faith of the participant, yet is not as true an illustration of the Papal doctrine as the one of medicine given to a patient, which has been employed in the text above.

did not dig deep enough. He insisted, it is true, on faith in the recipient; without which no benefit could be derived from the sacrament. But he nevertheless erroneously thought that there always was an inherent virtue in the sacrament, and that this inherent virtue was always communicated by the administration of the ordinance, although not always received by the person to whom the ordinance was administered. Its reception by this person depended upon his own faith. To illustrate his view of the subject, Luther brought forward the case of the woman with the issue of blood, who touched the hem of Jesus' garment, and was healed. There was real healing power in Christ, even though she had not touched him; but it needed her faith, which prompted the putting forth of the hand, in order that she should receive any benefit. So he argued it is with the sacraments: there is real efficacy in them, whether we are in a condition to receive it or not;

but we cannot receive it without faith. Now it will be readily seen by the careful thinker, that Luther's illustration does not cover the point in question. To make it pertinent, the healing power elicited by the faith of the diseased woman must be shown to have been resident not only in Christ, but in his garment which she touched—a proposition which even Luther would not attempt to maintain.

The *Reformed* doctrine on this subject, which we hold in common with almost all Protestants, is antagonistic to the Lutheran as well as to the Romish view. According to it, there is no efficacy whatever in the sacraments themselves, no saving virtue inherent in them, any more than there was healing power in the garment which Christ wore. The benefit which the recipient of the sacrament derives is not owing to any virtue in the sacrament, but to the accompanying power of the Holy Ghost: just as the woman was healed, not by the medicinal virtue of Christ's garment, but by the power of the great Physician himself, consciously exerted by him in response to her act of faith. The sacraments have, indeed, "an inherent moral power as significant emblems suggestive of the truth; but any supernatural effect which they produce is, according to the Reformed doctrine, to be referred exclusively to the power of the Holy Ghost, who works by them."

The Rev. Dr. Hodge of Princeton remarks on this subject as follows: "The theoretical difference between the Romish, Lutheran and Reformed doctrines, though it may seem, and often is represented, as of little account, since all ascribe supernatural effects to the sacraments, and all profess to require some subjective preparation in the recipient in order to their saving efficacy, *is*, however, as shown in history or by experience, of the greatest practical importance. The Romish doctrine, by requiring nothing but a negative condition on the part of the receiver, makes salvation a mechanical or magical process, carried on without any spiritual change in those on whom it confers eternal life. The Lutherans, on the other hand, by demanding a living faith, are saved from that evil; but, by making the sacraments inherently powerful, and grace inseparable from them, have unduly advanced their importance and necessity. . . . Luther at first said, the sacrament does nothing, but faith in the sacrament; though afterward, and in his larger catechism as well as elsewhere, he taught that faith does not make the sacrament, but apprehends the grace which is annexed to the outward sign. This means that, as the sacrament does not avail without faith, so faith does not avail without the sacrament."*

The Reformed doctrine, as it is clearly stated in our catechisms, is, that "the sacraments become effectual means of

* MS. Lectures to Students.

salvation, not by any power in themselves, or any virtue derived from the piety or intention of him by whom they are administered;"* "but only by the blessing of Christ, and the working of his Spirit in them that by faith receive them."† This view, however, while it condemns as erroneous any undue exaltation of the inherent efficacy of the sacraments, holds no fellowship, on the other hand, with the Socinian heresy, which would degrade them into mere Christian ceremonies designed simply as declarations of faith, and in which Christians are to be agents but not recipients: for they are held to be, by Christ's blessing and the Holy Spirit's working in them, "*effectual means of salvation;*" and by them, "Christ and the benefits of the new covenant" are not only "represented," but also "*sealed* and *applied* to believers."

* Larger Cat., qu. 161.   † Shorter Cat., qu. 91.

Design, Efficacy, and Mode of Baptism.

"*Go ye therefore, and teach all nations, baptizing them in the name of the Father, and of the Son, and of the Holy Ghost: teaching them to observe all things whatsoever I have commanded you: and, lo, I am with you alway, even unto the end of the world. Amen.*"—MATTHEW xxviii. 19, 20.

"*That he might sanctify and cleanse it with the washing of water by the word.*"—EPH. v. 26.

"*As many of you as have been baptized into Christ have put on Christ.*"—GAL. iii. 27.

"*Having our hearts sprinkled from an evil conscience, and our bodies washed with pure water.*"—HEB. x. 22.

CHAPTER II.

Design, Efficacy and Mode of Baptism.

BAPTISM of Jewish proselytes prior to the Christian era—an unauthorized, yet significant appendage to Circumcision.—General expectation in the Jewish mind that both Christ and his forerunner would baptize.—Examination of the time when Christian baptism commenced.—John's baptism not Christian baptism.—His baptism, like himself, belonged to the old dispensation.—The baptism performed by Christ's disciples prior to the resurrection not Christian baptism.—Baptism of three thousand on the day of Pentecost, the first Christian baptism.

The *design* of baptism. It is a symbol of purification, and suggests needed inward cleansing by the Holy Spirit.—Immersion theory not tenable.

The *efficacy* of baptism. God's signet to attest his promise.—Promise sure where all the conditions of it are fulfilled.

The *mode* of Christian baptism. Sprinkling, pouring and immersion, each valid.—The last the least significant and appropriate of the three modes.—No proof that immersion was ever practiced in the apostolic Church—on the contrary, much to show that baptism was usually, if not always, by either pouring or sprinkling.—Arguments against immersion as the exclusive mode.

BAPTISM was not first practiced by Christ, or by his forerunner, John. As a mode of initiation into discipleship, as a significant rite by which converts testified their reception of a new faith, it seems to have been employed before the Christian era. There is satisfactory evidence that proselytes to the Jewish religion from among the surrounding pagan nations, for a considerable time previous to the advent of Christ, had been baptized as well as circumcised.*

This practice of appending baptism to circumcision rested, indeed, upon no divine command; but gradually grew up, until at length it became a frequent, if not a uniformly practiced custom. In this connection it will be instructive also to notice a corresponding fact in regard to that other

---

* Jahn's Bib. Arch., p. 413: Mosheim, Com. on Hist. 1st 3 cent., vol. i., p. 89.

Jewish Church ordinance, the passover. Among the later Jews it had become the settled custom to drink four cups of red wine at the passover, although in the institution of this feast wine was not enjoined, nor in its original celebration used. We may see, however, the wisdom of God in these apparently trivial circumstances. In each case what, as an unauthorized outgrowth or addition, formed only a useless appendage to a holy ordinance given to the single nation of ancient Israel, was destined to become the appointed symbol of another holy ordinance of higher import, to be celebrated by all who in every nation should constitute the true Israel of God.

By one custom—corrupt, indeed, so far as strict Judaism was concerned, but providentially designed to form a beautiful connecting link between the symbols of the old and the new dispensation—the wine was present with the bread at the last paschal feast eaten under divine sanction, and was thus ready prepared to Jesus' hand for the institution of that simpler memorial ordinance of the Lord's Supper, which was to supersede the passover. By another custom—equally discordant with strict Judaism, yet certainly equally providential in its design to connect the two dispensations—baptism of proselytes had come to be a familiar thing; and so the way had been opened for the natural and easy adoption of baptism by Christ, as a simpler initiatory ordinance for his Church, in place of the rite of circumcision, to which it had become appended. Thus, in connection with each of the two Church sacraments, there had been gradual preparation for a change; and in both the change consisted in the laying aside of all that typified the necessity of a bloody sacrifice yet to be made, and in the retaining only of what should evermore symbolize the justifying power and the sanctifying grace of the one all-sufficient sacrifice already made.

Another important step in this preparatory process must not go unnoticed. The already introduced custom of baptizing proselytes to Judaism made it natural for the Jews to expect that any one who could substantiate his claims to being a teacher and reformer sent of God would baptize those whom he discipled. Accordingly, we find that when the priests and Levites were sent on a mission of inquiry to John the Baptist, they first questioned him as to whether he was the expected Messiah, or some mighty prophet of Jehovah; and not until he had answered in the negative, simply claiming to be "the voice of one crying in the wilderness, Make straight the way of the Lord,"* did they at all question his right to baptize. When, however, John (perhaps from ignorance that he was really that "Elias which was for to come"†) had discarded all claim to the prophetical office, they demanded of him, "Why bap-

* John i. 23.   † Matt. xi. 14.

tizest thou, then, if thou be not that Christ, nor Elias, neither that prophet?"

The question asked, it will be observed, was not as to the signification of the ceremony of baptism, as if it were a new rite, introduced for the first time by John, but as to his authority for performing this ceremony. It was a virtual inquiry why he, a private man and no prophet, should arrogate the right to set himself up as a public teacher, to organize a new sect of religionists, and to apply to his disciples, obtained from among his own countrymen, the Jews, that rite of initiation which had been customarily employed when pagans became Jews. But more than this seems to be implied in their question. It evidently indicates that there was a general expectation among the Jews that both the anticipated Messiah, and Elias his forerunner, would baptize men with water; and Mosheim has rightly interpreted it when he says that if the words spoken by the messengers be attentively considered, " they will unquestionably admit of the following construction: 'We, as well as those who sent us, understand that when the Messiah shall come, he will baptize and purify the Jewish race with water; we also expect that Elias, who is to precede him, will use the same ceremony for our initiation; but by what authority is it that you, who acknowledge that you are neither the Messiah nor Elias, assume to yourself the right of doing that which can only properly belong to them to perform—we do not mean the baptizing of strangers, but the descendants of Abraham?'"*

How this idea arose and became so prevalent there is no means of ascertaining. But it was a very remarkable and happy coincidence of circumstances, which favored the adoption by Christ of this emblem of purification as the initiatory ordinance of his church:—first, the growing

* Mosh. Com. vol. i., p. 90.

up of proselyte baptism into a customary appendage of circumcision; and, secondly, the turning of the popular mind of the nation toward baptism as a ceremony which was to be employed by the Messiah.

Just at this point, and before entering upon the main theme to be considered in this chapter—*the design, efficacy and mode of Christian baptism*—it is necessary to consider, briefly, *at what point of time* Christian baptism commences; which will involve also the important question whether either John's baptism or the baptism performed by Christ's disciples before his death is to be regarded as Christian baptism. Now, Christian baptism is that baptism which introduces the baptized persons into Christ's visible Church; and therefore we should expect to find an account of the regular organization of the Christian Church, either before or contemporaneously with the notice of the baptism of any into membership with it. But we have no such account prior to the death of Christ. On the contrary, we have the clearest proof that such an organization did not take place until the day of Pentecost. Not till then did the Holy Ghost descend upon the apostles, qualifying them for the great responsibility of such organization; and, according to the direction of Christ, they awaited his descent. No Christian baptism, therefore, could possibly have been administered before the day of Pentecost.

But, waiving this argument, and examining John's baptism on its own merits, it will be evident—

1. That John did not baptize "in the name of the Father and of the Son and of the Holy Ghost,"* according to the formula prescribed by Jesus to be used in administering Christian baptism.

2. That his baptism, in distinction from Christian baptism, is called the "baptism of repentance,"† a confession of sins being

---

* Mat. xxviii. 19. † Acts xix. 4.

all that he required from those who desired baptism at his hands.

3. That there is not the least shadow of probability that all the vast multitudes who flocked to him for baptism appreciated the true spiritual character of the Messiah, and placed a confiding trust in him as their Saviour from sin and death; or that their baptism was at all conditioned on their thus professing Christ: and yet, without such profession at the least, there could be no Christian baptism.

From all these reasons it would appear conclusive that John's baptism is not to be accounted Christian baptism. And in like manner we must judge of the baptism which Christ's disciples administered while he was with them—a ceremony evidently closely resembling John's baptism. No intimation is given that they baptized in the name of the Trinity; and there is nothing to show that the immense numbers of people baptized by them (at one time exceeding even the multitudes whom John baptized*) were afterward associated with them as Christian brethren. But, returning to the consideration of John's baptism, we have—.

4. A *positive* proof that it was not Christian baptism. This proof is found in the nineteenth chapter of the Acts of the Apostles, the first seven verses, which read as follows: " And it came to pass, that while Apollos was at Corinth, Paul, having passed through the upper coasts, came to Ephesus; and finding certain disciples, he said unto them, Have ye received the Holy Ghost since ye believed? And they said unto him, We have not so much as heard whether there be any Holy Ghost. And he said unto them, Unto what then were ye baptized? And they said, Unto John's baptism." Baptized unto John's baptism, and yet they had "*not so much as heard*" of the *existence*, not to say of the operations,

* John iv. 1, 2.

of the third person in the sacred Trinity! John did not then baptize "in the name of the Father and of the Son and of the Holy Ghost." Indeed, as soon as they told Paul in what manner they had been baptized, he understood their case at once, and said, "John verily baptized with the baptism of repentance, saying unto the people that they should believe on him which should come after him, that is, on Christ Jesus. When they heard this, they were baptized *in the name of the Lord Jesus;*" that is, probably, according to the formula given by the Lord Jesus. "And when Paul had laid his hands on them, the Holy Ghost came on them, and they spake with tongues, and prophesied. And all of the men were about twelve."

Surely, no more certain and explicit testimony than this could be desired, concerning the point we are considering. Here were twelve persons who had been previously baptized unto John's baptism, but who were now baptized into Christ. One of two things must be true: either their former baptism was not Christian baptism, or they *twice* received Christian baptism, and that, too, under the direct sanction of an Apostle. But, as the latter alternative cannot for a moment be supposed, the former must be the true one, and John's baptism must be pronounced to be *not Christian baptism.*

If, however, as appears manifest, it was not Christian baptism, what place does it hold in the divine economy of the Church? Why, undoubtedly the same place among church *rites* that John himself held among church *prophets.* He was not a prophet of the new, but of the old dispensation;—the last of the line, and pointing directly to Christ, who was to inaugurate the new order. So, also, his baptism was a ceremony not of the new, but of the old dispensation, though it was the last relic of that dispensation, and pointed with peculiar significance to the new.

Nor can the personal history of our Lord while here on earth, or that of his disciples while attendant upon his ministry, be said properly to belong to the new dispensation. He and they subjected themselves to all the requirements of the old Mosaic ritual; and it was not until his death that the types and shadows were fully done away, and the reality of a perfected redemption was offered to the world. Hence the baptism performed by his disciples prior to his death, like the baptism of John, partook of the nature of a *type*, looking forward to that complete purifying agency of the Holy Spirit yet to be provided by the atonement on Calvary. It did not possess the character of a pure *symbol*, significant of the ever-present regenerating power of the Holy Spirit, provided by an atonement already wrought out.

Furthermore, we have no account of the baptism of the one hundred and twenty disciples who formed the nucleus of the first

Christian Church, and who waited in Jerusalem for the descent of the Holy Spirit; nor of some of the original twelve. It is altogether probable, therefore, from all the data we have, that the first organization of the Church of Christ consisted of the apostles and of such others of Christ's former disciples as had truly appreciated him to be the Son of God, had believed on him as such, and to whom he had imparted his Spirit:—that these were considered by the apostles as the Church without any formal rite of initiation:—that their organization into a *visible* Church was completed on the day of Pentecost, when the Holy Ghost descended in tongues of flame and sat upon each one of them, thus designating who were the true children of God;—and that the baptism prescribed by Christ began from that time to be used as the holy ordinance of initiation into the visible Christian Church.

In this view (which we believe has the

sanction of God's word) the baptism of the three thousand on the day of Pentecost was the *first* Christian baptism; and hence any baptism previously administered cannot be of binding authority with us in determining the design, the efficacy or the mode of that baptism which Christ instituted for his Church.

The way is now prepared for considering the *design* and *efficacy* of this sacrament. The original and acquired significance of the word "sacrament," and what is essential to constitute a Christian sacrament, have been developed in the introductory chapter, and it has been shown that our own standards, in accordance with the standards of all the Reformed churches, rightly teach that there are three essentials to every sacrament of the Christian Church:—

1. That it be an "ordinance instituted by Christ;"

2. That it employ "sensible" signs;

3. That in it "Christ and the benefits of the new covenant shall be represented, sealed and applied to believers."

Does baptism fulfill all these conditions? That it was instituted by Christ needs no argument, as it appears unmistakably from the command of Christ: "Go ye therefore, and teach all nations, baptizing them in the name of the Father, and of the Son, and of the Holy Ghost."*

That it employs sensible (or visible) signs no one will deny who has ever seen it performed either by sprinkling, pouring or immersion. The water (however used) is certainly a visible sign of something. In this all Protestants, and even the Papists, agree. But of *what* is it the sign? What invisible grace is represented by the visible symbol? And in what sense, if at all, can the ordinance be said to seal and to apply the grace which it represents? On these

---

* Matt. xxviii. 19.

questions there is not so general an agreement. Yet it is very important that correct answers should be given to them; for a right understanding of the design and efficacy of baptism will go far toward a right decision as to its mode, while erroneous views here will almost certainly lead to erroneous conclusions as to the mode.

The Rev. J. Newton Brown, a Baptist clergyman, and editor of the "Encyclopedia of Religious Knowledge," says in that work: "The principal and most comprehensive design of this ordinance appears from the Scriptures to be a *solemn public and practical profession of Christianity.*" This I readily concede to be one main element in the design; but it must not be forgotten that, in the covenant entered into at baptism, there are two contracting parties, God and the baptized person; and that while the latter, by receiving baptism, makes a public profession of his faith in Christ, no less does God, by the authorized administration of the rite in his name, publicly pledge himself to grant whatever blessings are signified by the outward symbol. It is therefore important to ascertain with accuracy *what* invisible grace is symbolized by the visible sign.

Now, the natural and primary idea which the use of water in the symbol suggests is *purification*. The outward application of water to anything, and in any form, is naturally significant of *cleansing*. When applied to the body of a person, it is most commonly in order to cleanse away the impurities of the flesh. This idea of cleansing or purifying is undoubtedly the thought which would occur to the uninstructed mind of a pagan who, without any knowledge of the religious use of the ceremony, should see baptism for the first time administered, whether in its administration the candidate were plunged beneath the water, or the water were poured or sprinkled upon the candidate. The first impression in either case would be that of washing, in order to make pure. There is a world-wide conviction of impurity in the flesh, and a world-wide knowledge of the fact that water can remove this impurity. There is an equally world-wide impression of *spiritual* impurity. God hath written indelibly upon every heart a sense of moral defilement. Hence it is that the Hindoo bathes himself in the waters of the Ganges, to him sacred:—he thinks thereby to wash away the stains upon his soul. Hence, in all probability, arose that custom among the Jews, already considered, of adding baptism to circumcision in the case of pagan proselytes, as expressive of the fact that they needed a purification before they were worthy to be admitted among the number of God's chosen people. And hence, also, we have a natural solution of the general expectation which had grown up in the Jewish mind, that the Messiah at his coming would baptize even the circumcised Israelites, as a symbol of his cleansing them anew, to prepare them for the Messianic kingdom to be set up (as they supposed) at once on earth. Beautifully coincident with these world-wide convictions of impurity, and with these longings and expectations respecting the Messiah, is the evident design of Christian baptism, that, by the outward application of water in the ceremony, *the needed inward cleansing of the Holy Spirit* may be fitly represented and symbolized.

How it exalts our admiration of the Saviour, who in all things conformed his religion to the circumstances of mankind, that he should, even in the very symbols employed in the sacraments of his Church, speak at once to the senses of the unlettered savage and the long-taught Jew—should appeal to the inmost convictions of the blinded skeptic as well as of the believing disciple! For we maintain that it is not in the power of the most degraded or the most infidel of our species to see either of the sacramental ordinances of Christ's Church performed without being impressed with some sense of its significance. The bread and the wine, partaken of by the communicants at the Lord's table, must speak to him of nourishment and gladness; the washing with water in the sacrament of baptism cannot fail to tell him of a design to cleanse. True, if his conceptions are all carnal, he will behold in the one only the feasting of the body, and in the other only the cleansing of the flesh; but just so soon as he obtains any spiritual conception of the ceremonies, naturally and without instruction will he embrace the idea of a spiritual feasting and of a spiritual cleansing. And it would be well for those who make baptism primarily to signify a burial, or a death, or any other thing than a purification, to consider that in so doing they are declaring open war against the God-implanted instincts of the whole human race.

Whatever interpretation the *Bible* puts upon this symbol is, of course, authoritative, yet the Bible generally will be found to speak in harmony with universal consciousness, and we should always be very cautious in deciding that its testimony is otherwise. A most careful and extended examination of God's word in regard to the subject under consideration has fully convinced the writer that there is nothing in it contradictory to the idea that baptism primarily symbolizes cleansing, while there is an abundance of Scripture to confirm this idea. Without pausing here for more extended quotations, two passages may be cited from the Old Testament and two from the New: the former to show that, under God's appointment, in the Mosaic ritual, water was used as an emblem of purification; and the latter to show that, under Christ's appointment, in the ordinance of baptism, it possesses the same signification. Ex. xxix. 4: "Aaron and his sons thou shalt bring unto the door of the tabernacle of the congregation, and shalt wash them with water." Num. viii. 5-7: "The Lord spake unto Moses, saying, Take the Levites from among the children of Israel, and cleanse them. And thus shalt thou do unto them to cleanse them: sprinkle water of purifying upon them, and let them shave all their flesh, and let them wash their clothes, and so make themselves clean." Eph. v. 25-27: "Christ also loved the Church, and gave himself for it: that he might sanctify and cleanse it with the washing of water, by the word, that he might present it to himself a glorious Church, not having spot or wrinkle, or any such thing: but that it should be holy and without blemish." Titus iii. 5: "According to his mercy he saved us, by the washing of regeneration, and renewing of the Holy Ghost."

Such, as we understand it, is the symbolic import of baptism. And to this view we believe no exception is taken by any of the societies or members of the Church catholic, except by those who contend that immersion is the only mode of baptism. With them baptism is made to represent the *burial and resurrection* of our Lord; and the principal passages relied upon for the support of this view are Rom. vi. 4, and Col. ii. 12: in both of which occurs the phrase, " Buried with him by (or in) baptism." This burial, they say, is symbolized by the *immersion* of the body in water; and the resurrection alluded to in the same connection, by the *raising up* of the body again from the water.

To such a theory it may be objected:—

1. That (as already said) it contradicts the universal consciousness of mankind, which always attaches to water the idea of cleansing.

2. That it contradicts Jehovah's express sanction to this idea in the typical use to which water was applied under the old dispensation.

3. That it destroys the significance of the many beautiful comparisons made in the New Testament between the outward application of water to the body and the inward application of God's Spirit to the soul.

4. That it takes away the symbol from the ordinance as a whole, and attaches it to a specific mode of administering the ordinance; making the symbolic intent to rest altogether in the manner in which the ceremony is performed, and not at all in the substance with which it is done. Under this idea immersion in any other fluid (as oil, for example) would be as significant as immersion in water.

5. That it is clearly contradictory to the fair and impartial interpretation of the only two passages of Scripture which are urged in its support. These passages are the ones to which reference has already been made. That in Col. ii. 12 will be seen, by a careful examination of its context, to have reference to Christ's *death* rather than to

his burial; and that in Rom. vi. 4 explicitly says, "Buried with him by baptism into *death:*" explained by the verse preceding, "Baptized into *his* death." The main design of the apostle then evidently is, "to show, that, by the solemn profession made at baptism, Christians become dead to sin, as Christ was dead to the living world around him when he was buried." Possibly there may be an allusion in the form of speech used to the custom of baptizing by immersion, which, in that warm climate, may have been a not unfrequent mode. But there is no necessity of supposing even such an allusion. Persons baptized by pouring or by sprinkling water upon them are just as truly and really baptized into the death of Christ as those who are immersed. They are just as truly buried with him in their profession of death to sin; and by faith, just as truly raised again to a life of holiness. The death and the burial and the resurrection here spoken of are all *spiritual*, and ought not to be degraded to a literal and physical interpretation, any more than in the fifth verse, where it is said, "We have been *planted together.*" Would any man attempt to carry this out on the same principle of exact, literal interpretation? But we forbear, for this branch of the subject has already received a larger share of attention than at first intended. Surely no unprejudiced mind, after a careful consideration of the arguments presented in the discussion thus far, can fail to be convinced that the primary thing symbolized in baptism is *not a burial*, but a *purification* or a *cleansing*.

This purification must be wrought in us by the mighty power of God. Nothing else can cleanse us from sin. It is the special work of the Holy Spirit, by whose agency Christ is formed in us, first to justify and then to sanctify. The Holy Spirit alone can regenerate. But regeneration is essential to salvation, and without it no man can become a member of the invisible body of Christ. Therefore the initiatory ordinance to Christ's visible body, the Church, was designedly and most appropriately made to symbolize regeneration.

If such, then, be the design of baptism, what is its *efficacy?* In what sense may it be said *to seal and to apply* the grace of regeneration, which it represents? That it is the *seal* of this grace is evident from all the arguments adduced to prove that it is the sign or symbol of it. Also by the fact that the ordinance is administered, by Christ's delegated authority, " in the name of the Father, and of the Son, and of the Holy Ghost," thus pledging the sacred Trinity, as it were, in a solemn covenant with the believing recipient of the ordinance. And again, since baptism occupies the same position under the covenant of grace that circumcision did under the Abrahamic covenant, and since circumcision is declared in Rom. iv. 11, to be "*a seal of the righteousness of the faith*" which Abraham had—that is, of the righteousness which became his by faith, for he was justified by faith, and not by works—therefore this passage is at once a proof and an explanation of the fact that baptism is a seal as well as a sign. It is God's *signet*, set to the promise of his grace, attesting his promise to the believing recipient. But faith is an essential requisite. Without faith, the sacrament of baptism will be only a dead ceremony. With faith, it is the seal of the Almighty.

And will the unchangeable God be slack to perform the thing which he promises, and to which he affixes his seal? If not, then where the blessing is sealed it is also *applied*. In other words, the invisible grace of regeneration is sure to be communicated to those who with true faith receive the visible sign of it. The word of God confirms this in Gal. iii. 27, in the declaration, "As many of you as have been baptized into Christ have put on Christ." This does not, however, inculcate the Roman Catholic error of baptismal regeneration; that is, that baptism has power in itself to renew the unbelieving soul, just as a medicine has to heal the sick; nor the Lutheran error, which makes regeneration inseparable from baptism, so that no one can be saved without being baptized. Both these are contrary to the Scripture, "He that believeth and is baptized shall be saved; but he that believeth not shall be damned."* In this declaration of our Lord, given by Mark in connection with the last commission to the apostles, three things are noticeable:—

1. Faith and baptism are declared certain to secure salvation.

2. Absence of faith is declared damning.

3. Absence of baptism is not so declared. Hence this Scripture, taken in connection

* Mark xvi. 16.

with the declarations elsewhere, "Believe on the Lord Jesus Christ, and thou shalt be saved;"* "Christ is the end of the law for righteousness to every one that believeth,"† would seem to show conclusively that salvation is possible without baptism. Thus, a man cast upon a desert island by shipwreck, though he has lived a lifetime in sin, has never been baptized, and cannot there be, yet if he truly repents and believes in Christ, his faith will save him. "The ancient Church, therefore," as remarked by an able commentator, "was perfectly correct in acknowledging even unbaptized persons who, during the persecutions, had confessed Christ, and been put to death in consequence, to be true believers. But had these confessors remained alive, obedience to the command of the Lord would have impelled them to seek baptism."‡

* Acts xvi. 31.   † Rom. x. 4.
‡ Ols. Com. vol. iv., p. 298, n. 1.

Baptism is not essential to salvation in the same sense as faith, as being an indispensable means to an end (a *sine qua non* to getting to heaven); but it is essential as a command of our divine Master. There is high import in the fact that Jesus has commanded all nations to be baptized as well as to be discipled, and that he has linked baptism with faith in the stipulated condition upon which he promises salvation. Those, therefore, who causelessly neglect to be baptized, or who, if baptized in infancy, neglect to ratify this baptism by a public confession of their faith, do so at their peril. There is no reason to expect God's favor so long as we despise a plain command of Christ, or comply only partially with the declared terms on which his favor may be secured.

The way is now prepared to enter understandingly upon a consideration of the *mode* of Christian baptism. Must it be *always by immersion?* Or, is baptism by *sprinkling* or *pouring* equally valid?

For it must be remembered that there is no dispute whatever about the validity of immersion as a mode. All Christians agree that baptism by immersion (if in all other particulars rightly performed) is valid. But our Church, in common with other pedobaptist churches, believe that baptism by sprinkling or by pouring is equally valid; and that the mode in which water is applied to the person is not at all essential in order to validity. On the ground of *appropriateness*, however, we maintain that either pouring or sprinkling is preferable to immersion, since the blessings which come to us by faith are thereby more aptly symbolized. Thus, in 1 Pet. i. 2 we have, "The *sprinkling* of the blood of Jesus Christ;" in Heb. x. 22, "Our hearts *sprinkled* from an evil conscience, and our bodies washed with pure water;" in Acts

ii. 17, "I will *pour out* of my spirit upon all flesh;" in Acts x. 45, "On the Gentiles also was *poured out* the gift of the Holy Ghost;" and a multitude of other passages of like import.

But the issue, and the only real issue as to mode, is whether any other mode than immersion is valid. And this issue our Baptist brethren force upon us, by laying claim to immersion as the exclusive mode, and by unchurching all who have not been immersed.

Let us examine into the merits of their claim. And,

1. It is to be observed that *John's* example is no authority on this subject, as has been clearly shown in the first part of this chapter. If, therefore, it could be positively proved that John always baptized by immersion, this would not at all bind us to that mode. It would have its effect by way of illustration of the probability, in the absence of anything definite or positive,

just as the proselyte baptism of the Jews would; but nothing more. Hence, even if it could be shown by evidence perfectly satisfactory, that all of John's disciples and even our Lord himself were immersed, our opinion of the validity of other modes of baptism would be unchanged; because, it rests on facts which would still remain unshaken. It is, however, a matter of serious question whether all, or even a majority, of those whom John baptized were immersed. Indeed, it cannot be proved conclusively that he ever immersed a single one; and it is altogether probable, from the great multitudes who resorted to him, that he customarily *poured* water upon their heads while they stood in the brink of the river, according to the mode which we find "depicted on the most ancient Christian monuments."* As to that oft-quoted proof-passage which says he baptized "in Enon near to Salim, because

* Hodge's MS. Lect.

there was *much water* there,"* it reads in the original Greek "*many waters*," and means undoubtedly many water-springs or small rivulets, rendering the place a desirable and well-chosen one, in order that the vast numbers who came to John might be furnished with drink, etc. But grant that John always immersed, and, as has been said, it will by no means prove that *Christian* baptism was by immersion, and by immersion only, in the Apostolic Church.

2. The whole analogy of the Christian dispensation forbids a rigid adherence to any precise form, except where it is part of the very essence of the thing. The words, "in the name of the Father, and of the Son, and of the Holy Ghost,"† must always be used as a formula in baptizing, because this is the explicit command of Jesus; and because it is an essential recognition of the Trinity as a party to the covenant. But, with reference to the quantity of water to be used; or

* John. iii. 23.   † Matt. xxviii. 19.

whether it should be applied to the whole body, or only to a part of it; or as to the particular part to which it should be applied; Christ gave no directions whatever when he instituted the ordinance. On another occasion, however, previous to this, he had laid down a rule which, applied here, will show that all these matters are perfectly nonessential. When he washed the disciples' feet, and when Peter, in his impulsive zeal, turned immersionist and demanded a complete and entire ablution, Christ informed him, "He that is washed, needeth not save to wash his feet, but is clean every whit." And if water applied to the *feet* only is a sufficient emblem of perfect purification, is it not equally so when applied to the *head?* The symbolic intent of baptism, as has already been shown in speaking of the design of the ordinance, requires that water shall in some form be applied to the person as an emblem of purification. But the *mode* of its application is *not indicated*, and is evidently *entirely immaterial*. As the Lord's Supper may be eaten with bread leavened or unleavened; with wine fermented or unfermented; in a sitting, kneeling, reclining or standing posture; at evening (the time when the passover was eaten, and when the Lord's Supper was instituted) or in the morning; in an upper chamber or in a church; so may baptism be administered by either of the three modes under discussion.

3. The *example of the apostles* and of their co-workers seems to be *uniformly against immersion*. It cannot, indeed, be positively shown that they never did immerse, although, from all that is in the New Testament, it is quite probable that they never did. That the first Christian baptism, administered to three thousand persons on the day of Pentecost, should have been by immersion is almost impossible to conceive, even judging by the simple narrative itself; for the whole one hundred

and twenty disciples there assembled would scarcely have been able to perform the rite in one day, after the long preceding services of the day were ended; and besides, in a hostile city, where the chief priests and elders were all against the little Christian band, even if there had been an abundance of water in the city, it could only have been by a miracle as great as any other which was wrought on that day of wonders, that one hundred and twenty fonts large enough for immersing should have been accessible to the disciples. But the late Rev. Dr. Robinson, who twice journeyed over Palestine making the most minute inspections, and whose printed researches are quoted as authority by every scholar, says, "Against the idea of full immersion there lies a difficulty, apparently insuperable, in the scarcity of water. There is in summer (and this baptism took place in June) no running stream in the vicinity of Jerusalem, except the mere rill of Siloam a few rods in length; and the city is and was supplied from its cisterns and public reservoirs."* Neither of these sources, he concludes, could have furnished a sufficient supply for the immersing of these three thousand, and of five thousand more mentioned in Acts iv. 4, as added to the believers, even if we suppose the time of baptism to have been extended to several days after conversion. And he adds, "The same scarcity of water forbade the use of private baths as a general custom."

For the same reasons already presented, the learned Dr. Olshausen of Germany yields the point that the baptism in this case could not have been by immersion, although this confession is opposed to his idea that immersion was the usual practice of the early Church. He says, "It is difficult, however, to answer the question how the baptism of three thousand persons could be performed in one day, according to the

* Rob. Grk. Lex., art Ba----.

old practice of a complete submersion, the more especially as in Jerusalem there was no water at hand with the exception of Kidron and a few pools. But to have baptized so many persons in these would necessarily have excited in the highest degree the attention of the authorities. The difficulty can only be removed by supposing that they *already employed mere sprinkling*, or that they baptized in houses in tubs; formal submersion in rivers or larger quantities of water probably took place only where the locality conveniently allowed it."* But, again let it be noticed, there is *no proof* that formal submersion *ever* took place in the Apostolic Church.

The next mention of baptism in the New Testament history of the Church is that of the Samaritans by Philip, in which no circumstances aid us to form an opinion as to the mode. The next is Philip's baptism of the eunuch, the mode of which has been

* Com. on Acts ii. 37–41; n. i. p. 383.

much disputed, and it is barely possible that it was by immersion. If so, here is one solitary known case to offset against the eight thousand whom we have already seen must have been baptized in some other way. Our translation, "They went down both into the water," and they came "up out of the water," is fully sustained by the Greek text. But giving the prepositions the full force claimed for them, we are by no means compelled to accept the inference that the baptism was by immersion. No violence is done to the language of the narrative by supposing that either pouring or sprinkling was the method here employed; as will be readily seen by reading literally the two sentences giving an account of the baptism, with an added clause between declaring by what mode it was done. "And they went down both into the water, both Philip and the eunuch, and he baptized him" by dipping water from the little rivulet or pool, with a cup or with his hand,

and by pouring or sprinkling it on his head, as they stood thus together in the water. "And when they were come up out of the water, the Spirit of the Lord caught away Philip, that the eunuch saw him no more."

This is much more in harmony with all the circumstances than to suppose the baptism to have been by complete submersion. It was "desert"* country through which they were passing, containing *no large* streams or fountains sufficient for immersing; and besides, as the eunuch was on a journey, and went on his way again immediately without any change of apparel so far as appears, the probabilities are all against his being immersed, even had there been an ample supply of water for the purpose.

The next instance is the baptism of St. Paul by Ananias, which is narrated in these words: "And he received sight forthwith, and *arose and was baptized.*"

* Acts viii. 26.

That is, as would naturally appear, he was baptized as soon as he arose, or while standing there in the house, in the place where Ananias found him. Not a hint at immersion—nothing that looks like it—on the contrary, the circumstances apparently against it.

The next recorded case is that of Cornelius and his Gentile friends, whom Peter commanded to be baptized. And here again nothing goes to prove or even to favor immersion. The question which Peter asked, "Can any man forbid water, that these should not be baptized?" has no reference to the *quantity* of water, but rather to the use of water at all for the baptism of *Gentiles*, as is clearly shown by the appended explanatory words, "*which have received the Holy Ghost as well as we.*" This added clause was evidently intended to explain the reason why the question was asked. Peter was accompanied by Jewish brethren. Here were

Gentiles evidently converted. He saw now what God meant to teach him by that precedent vision, and by the declaration, "What God hath cleansed, that call not thou common."* He was convinced that these Gentiles, having thus been made the subjects of the grace of God in conversion, and having received the gift of the Holy Ghost, were now fit subjects for baptism, although uncircumcised. But would his brethren of the circumcision, who had not been instructed as he had by a heavenly vision, agree with him in this, or would they object? He turns and asks them, "Can *any* man" (strict Jew though he be) "forbid water, that these should not be baptized, *which have received the Holy Ghost as well as we?*"† Do we need any further explanation of this case? We have it in the answer which Peter gave to "the apostles and brethren that were in Judea," when they afterward called him to an

* Acts x. 15. † Acts x. 47.

account for what he had here done. "Then remembered I," he says, "the word of the Lord, how that he said, John indeed baptized with water; but ye shall be baptized with the Holy Ghost:"—[who will dare to substitute *immerse* here, and say, "Ye shall be immersed with the Holy Ghost?"]—"Forasmuch then as God gave them the like gift as he did unto us, who believed on the Lord Jesus Christ, what was I, that I could withstand God?"*

The only other instance in the New Testament where any details are given is that of the jailer at Philippi. He and his whole household were baptized unexpectedly, and in the middle of the night. It is not at all likely that the mode was immersion. Such a supposition is forced and unnatural. The idea that water sufficient and accessible for the purpose was ready at hand on this occasion is altogether improbable, and not to be entertained without the most ample

* Acts xi. 17.

proof. And there is not the semblance of the shadow of such a proof.

4. Were it not for protracting this discussion beyond the limits prescribed for it, abundance of proof could be furnished that the Greek words *bapto* (βάπτω) and *baptidzo* (βαπτίζω), "to baptize," and *baptisma* (βάπτισμα), "baptism," were employed among the later Hellenistic Greeks in cases where it is impossible for them to mean "to immerse" and "immersion;" and hence they do not at all stand in the way of the view entertained by us.*

5. A strong incidental argument against the immersion theory might also be founded upon the great inconvenience and the *positive unsafety* of immersion, as a church

---

* Those who would like to acquaint themselves with the real meaning and use of these words, can find a lucid and satisfactory discussion of the Subject in "*Hall on Baptism*," published by the Presbyterian Publication Committee; and a still fuller handling of the subject in a recent issue entitled "*Classic Baptism*," by Dale.

rite, to be practiced in all climes and at all seasons.*

* Our Baptist brethren frequently are met with this practical obstacle in the way of their rigid views, as appears by the following pertinent testimony to the point, clipped from a weekly paper, issued since the above was written:

BAPTIZING IN WARM WATER.—A correspondent of the *Watchman and Reflector* (a Baptist paper) thus recounts a case of a female applicant for baptism: "I lost no time in conversing with her, and soon found that her piety was very decided, that her view of duty as to baptism was very clear, and that I could not 'forbid water that she should be baptized.' But a greater difficulty did exist, arising from the exceedingly delicate state of her health. On this matter I deemed it necessary to consult her physician, who, being an excellent Baptist deacon, fully sympathized with us in the whole matter. His frank statement was, 'If you baptize her in cold water, I consider it doubtful whether she will come out of the baptistery alive, but if you can conscientiously baptize her in warm or tepid water, I apprehend no danger.' To this proposal I could make no objection; one or two of the deacons, and a few of the female members of the church were called together, and sweet and solemn was the service we celebrated." On this the Boston *Recorder* remarks: "But suppose the minister, like some of our Baptist brethren, had thought the ordinance could be properly administered only in a running stream, what then? Why, the poor, delicate believer must have gone without this testi-

6. Finally, the continued and unmistakable sanction which God has given to pedobaptist churches for ages, in the gracious outpouring of his blessed Spirit upon them, ought for ever to silence all cavils against the validity of baptism performed either by sprinkling or pouring. It is the same divine attestation of God's approval which was given to Peter when he

mony of her faith. This case, and many others like it, furnish very strong collateral evidence against that view of the mode of baptism which reverses our Saviour's maxim, and makes him in effect to have 'come to destroy men's lives, and not to save them.' But doubtless new baptisteries will have furnace-pipes near or through them, to render the water 'warm or tepid.' This would be a wise and humane arrangement."

And yet another testimony of the same kind has come to us still later. It is a new item in one of our Western journals of the day, and is as follows:

"After being immersed, and while still in the river near St. Joseph, Mo., Oct. 18th (1868), a Mr. Stephens fell back and died almost instantly. Physicians say the sudden shock which the immersion gave to the nervous system caused syncope and death." . . . . So much for the standing miracle that "immersion hurts nobody."

first preached to and baptized the Gentiles at the house of Cornelius, and which caused him to say, "What was I, that I could withstand God?"

From all these arguments the conclusion is unavoidable with us that sprinkling and pouring are both valid modes of baptism—that either of these modes is more truly symbolic of what baptism is intended to teach than immersion is—that either of them is more appropriate than immersion, safer for all climates and all seasons, and hence more likely to be chosen of the Lord as a perpetually binding church rite—that nothing in God's Word forbids the selection of either of these modes in preference to immersion—and that the claim for immersion as the exclusive and only mode of baptism is entirely untenable, unscriptural and unsound.

Let us be prepared always to receive the truth in the love of it, whether it accords with our preconceived opinions or not.

And, above all, let us not forget that which is symbolized, in our earnest study of the symbol; but let us rise by faith to a higher and yet higher conception of what is spiritual; let us drink more and more largely of the Spirit of our divine Master, until, purified from all remains of corruption, we shall be wholly conformed to his spotless image.

The Proper Subjects of Baptism.

"*I will be a God unto thee and to thy seed.*"—GEN. xvii. 7.

"*The promise is unto you and to your children.*"—ACTS ii. 39.

"*Go ye therefore, and teach all nations, baptizing them.*"—MATT. xxviii. 19.

"*She was baptized, and her household.*"—ACTS xvi. 15.

"*And was baptized, he and all his, straightway.*"—ACTS xvi. 33.

"*I baptized also the household of Stephanas.*"—1 COR. i. 16.

"*Suffer the little children to come unto me, and forbid them not; for of such is the kingdom of God.*"—MARK x. 14.

[*See also parallel passages,* MATT. xix. 14, *and* LUKE xviii. 16.]

CHAPTER III.

The Proper Subjects of Baptism.

BAPTISM first—complete Indoctrination afterward.—Adults to confess Christ and be baptized as soon as they believe.—Infant children of believers also to receive baptism.—Such baptized children, Church members.—Our Standards teach this.—The Bible sanctions it.—Question as to female Infants.—Christ's commission to baptize intended to include Infants.—The Apostles so understood it, and accordingly baptized whole households.—Objections against Infant baptism considered and answered.—Evils springing from the failure of the Church to comprehend and act on the true doctrine.

IF the process of reasoning embraced in the preceding discussion is correct, then the three modes of baptism spoken of are equally valid; and *appropriateness* is the only thing to be considered in deciding which method in any given case shall be employed.

The next topic which naturally claims attention is the consideration of the *proper subjects* of baptism, or the question *to what persons* ought the ordinance to be administered?

The last commission of Christ to his apostles contains no specific direction on this point; yet the wording of this commission, when carefully studied, will not only furnish a clew to the true doctrine, but will, we think, be found to be wholly irreconcilable with any other. The whole commission, as given by Matthew (xxviii. 19, 20), reads: "Go ye therefore, and teach all nations, baptizing them in the name of the Father, and of the Son, and of the Holy Ghost; teaching them to observe all things whatsoever I have commanded you: and, lo, I am with you alway, even unto the end of the world. Amen." All scholars agree that the word translated "teach" in the first clause of this commission ("Go ye therefore, and teach all nations") means properly "to disciple" or "to make disciples of," and should be so rendered in the English. The reading would then be, "Go ye therefore, and *disciple* all nations," which reading is usually given in the margin of our reference Bibles. "Go *disciple* all nations"—make disciples or Christians of all nations. The remainder of the commission tells how this is to be done; viz., by "baptizing" and by "teaching." "Baptizing them in the name of the Father, and of the Son, and of the Holy Ghost," was to be the first process; "Teaching them to observe all things, whatsoever I have commanded you," the second, or finishing process. In order to the baptism of adults, it was of course necessary that they should possess a sufficient knowledge of gospel truth to be able understandingly to place all their trust in Jesus as their Saviour, as well as to believe in the existence and offices of the three persons of the Sacred Trinity. But their complete indoctrination, the perfecting of their instruction in the things of Christianity, was to take place after baptism. This plan was in harmony with the practice of our Lord as regards his twelve disciples. When he called them, they had faith enough to follow him, and to place confidence in him as their Leader and Master; but they were far from comprehending the full import of his mission. It took three years of his constant and most careful teaching to enable them to do this. And when they did thoroughly comprehend it, only eleven remained steadfast in the faith. One of the twelve, in the strong language of his Master, then proved himself a "devil."

The subsequent practice of the apostles followed the order of procedure which is here marked out for discipling the nations. All who were willing, on hearing their message, to profess faith in the Lord Jesus Christ were at once baptized, and then, subsequent to their baptism, a thorough course of instruction in the various doctrines of the gospel scheme was pursued; and if such more perfect instruction and longer trial should reveal the fact that any had been hypocritical in their first confession of the faith, this was with them no valid argument against pursuing the plan marked out by Christ. The gospel net was still to be drawn, and to gather up all that came in its way, good and bad alike, though, in the final assorting of characters from this net, the bad would be rejected, and the good only preserved to life eternal. Accordingly, on the day of Pentecost, many who that day listened for the first time to the gospel message were immediately received to the visible Church by baptism; yet we are told that "they continued" afterward "in the apostles' *doctrine*," or under the doctrinal instruction of the apostles, as well as " in fellowship and in breaking of bread and in prayers;"* and we are still farther

* Acts ii. 42.

informed, that at least two of the newly-received church members conspired to lie against the Holy Ghost, and were struck dead for their offence.* So, also, when the gospel was preached among the Samaritans by Philip, it is narrated of Simon the sorcerer that he "believed" and "was baptized;" but only a few days after he is told by Peter, "Thou hast neither part nor lot in this matter; for thy heart is not right in the sight of God."† It plainly appears from these examples, and from others which might be adduced, that, according to the interpretation given by the apostles to this last command of Christ, (an interpretation wholly accordant, as we have seen, with the evident import of the language of the command), we are not to wait for long years of trial before we receive converts into the visible Church. Nor are they to wait to master and comprehend all the Christian doctrines before presenting them-

---

* Acts chap. v. † Acts viii. 21.

selves to the Church, and becoming connected with the professed people of God. True faith in the Lord Jesus Christ is the gift of God, wrought in us by the effectual working of the Holy Ghost; and no man can believe in Christ, and take him as his Saviour, unless his heart is changed and he is a new creature. Hence, if any man feels that he does in reality believe in Christ, he has a right to conclude from that that he has been born again; and it becomes at once his bounden duty to declare himself on the Lord's side, by publicly entering into covenant relations with God's people. The Church, too, is bound to receive him so soon as he is ready to make confession of his faith, unless some open immorality, or some manifestly inconsistent action, or some evident defect in views, proclaims his unfitness and furnishes evidence of hypocrisy: and baptism is the initiatory ordinance, to be administered to him at his reception. But his Christian training is by no means completed when this sealing ceremony of his introduction into the Church has been performed. He is thenceforward to be more perfectly taught in all things whatsoever Christ has commanded. He must then commence, and ever after pursue, a searching into those "deep things" of God, some of which he will be able to comprehend here, and yet more will be reserved for his eternal study beyond the grave.

So much in reference to the baptism of adults. They are to be baptized only when they shall make a credible profession of their faith in the Lord Jesus Christ; and baptism is to them the rite of initiation into the visible Church. Thus far the different Protestant churches are in the main agreed; but we are now about to tread on disputed ground.

Our brethren of the Baptist denomination conscientiously restrict the administration of the ordinance to adult believers, while we as conscientiously hold that it is our privilege and our imperative duty to administer it also to the *children* of such believers. We believe that while the mode of baptism is entirely unimportant, *to believe in and to practice infant baptism is highly important*. Our Church standards demand it. It is as much a part of strict Presbyterianism as immersion is a part of the creed of the Baptist denomination. Thus, in our Confession of Faith, chap. xxviii., sec. 4, it is stated, " Not only those that do actually profess faith in and obedience unto Christ, but also the infants of one or both believing parents, are to be baptized." The 95th answer in the Shorter Catechism says: " The infants of such as are members of the visible Church are to be baptized." And the Directory for Worship, chap. vii., sec. 4, enjoins it upon ministers to teach, " that the seed of the faithful have *no less a right* to this ordinance under the gospel than the seed of

Abraham to circumcision under the Old Testament."

But an important question arises here. You have perceived that, in the progress of the discussion thus far, the position has been taken that this sacrament is an initiatory ordinance, by which persons are admitted into the visible Church. Is this position now to be abandoned?—or does it hold good with reference to infants as well as adults? In other words, are baptized children church members?

I answer, that it is our belief, and the unequivocal teaching of our standards, that they are just as really members of the visible Church as baptized adults are. Indeed, on no other ground can infant baptism be upheld. It inevitably stands or falls with the theory that the infant offspring of believing parents are included in God's covenant promises to those parents; and *on this account* are entitled to baptism, whereby they become connected with the visible organization of believers.

It is to be feared that many of our own church members have not given this subject the attention that it deserves, and it is not impossible that some who read these pages may suppose we are here advancing a *new* theory. The failure to place this doctrine of infant baptism on its true basis has, we fear, been the fruitful cause of much neglect on the part of parents in reference to this duty. It is all important, therefore, that the members in our own communion, at least, should know what our standards actually teach; and then that they should, after the example of the Bereans of old, " search the Scriptures daily, whether these things are so."

There need be no mistake here, for the utterance of our standards on this point is clear and explicit. Conf. Faith, chap. xxv., sec. 2 : " The visible Church consists of all those throughout the world that profess the true religion, *together with their children.*" The same is taught in the sixty-second answer of the Larger Catechism. Again, chap ii., sec. 2, Form of Gov't; " The universal Church consists of all those persons, in every nation, *together with their children*, who make profession of the holy religion of Christ, and of submission to his laws:" and sec. 4; " A particular church consists of a number of professing Christians, *with their offspring*, voluntarily associated together," etc. Answer 166, Larger Catechism, asserts that " Infants descending from parents, either both or but one of them professing faith in Christ and obedience to him, are, *in that respect, within the covenant*, and to be baptized." In chap. i., sec. 6, on Discipline, it is declared, " All baptized persons are members of the Church, are under its care, and subject to its government and discipline: and when they have arrived at the years of discretion, they are bound to perform all the duties of church members." And chap. ix., sec. 1, of Directory for Worship, declares that "Children, born within the pale of the visible Church, and dedicated to God in baptism, are under the inspection and government of the Church; and are to be taught to read, and repeat the catechism, the apostles' creed, and the Lord's prayer. They are to be taught to pray, to abhor sin, to fear God, and to obey the Lord Jesus Christ. And when they come to years of discretion, if they be free from scandal, appear sober and steady, and to have sufficient knowledge to discern the Lord's body, they ought to be informed it is their duty and their privilege to come to the Lord's Supper."

Such, then, is the teaching of the standards of the Presbyterian Church: and it might be proved by ample quotations, that similar doctrines with regard to the children of the Church are held by the Episcopal, the Reformed Dutch, the Methodist, and the Congregational churches. We by no means stand alone, nor are our views peculiar in this matter. But, leaving human declarations, let us turn to God's word, and examine this highest authority, to ascertain whether the views now presented have the *Divine* sanction to support them. We firmly believe they have. We cannot interpret the Bible in any other way than as allowing, and indeed imperatively requiring, the baptism of the infant offspring of professing Christians; thus giving them a place in the visible Church, "upon the supposition," as Dr. Watts expresses it, "of their being (with their parents) members of the invisible Church of God."* It seems to us impossible that the full import of Christ's command to disciple the nations, "baptizing them in the name of the Father, and of the Son, and of the Holy Ghost,"† can be complied with, except by administering baptism to the offspring of believing

---

* Bib. Rep., Jan. 1857, p. 23.   † Matt. xxviii. 19.

parents, as well as to the parents themselves. "Baptizing them." Notice that the pronoun *them* refers for its antecedent to the noun *nations* in the preceding clause, " Go disciple all nations, baptizing them." In order rightly to understand this direction, we must place ourselves on the standpoint occupied by the apostles when it was addressed to them. They were Jews, brought up under the Jewish economy; had been themselves received into the Jewish Church in infancy by the rite of circumcision; were accustomed to witness the reception of proselytes into that Church from the surrounding pagan nations, when all the males of the families so received were circumcised—infants and adults;* and now they are sent forth by Christ to make proselytes or disciples to his religion from among both Jews and Gentiles, even from all nations, and are told to baptize these proselytes, instead of circumcising them. Is it

* Ex. xii. 48.

for one moment to be presumed that they would interpret this charge to mean that they were to baptize only the adults? We maintain that nothing short of an explicit command *not* to baptize infants could have justified them in such an inference, as it would be directly contrary to all their former education and experience. In the absence, therefore, of any such command not to baptize infants, and acting under the commission given thus in general terms to " disciple the nations" and to " baptize them," their practice would undoubtedly, and as a matter of course, be to baptize the *entire households* of the new converts, just as they would formerly have circumcised all the males of those households, on their becoming proselytes to the Jewish faith.

A question, however, very fairly arises here, how *female* infants came to be baptized, without any explicit direction to that effect, since the rite of circumcision was applied only to males? But if this question afford any difficulty, that difficulty will lie in the case of adults equally as of infants; and the burden of its explanation will devolve as really upon those who oppose infant baptism as upon ourselves. The explanation usually adopted is that which is given by Calvin in the following words: "Nor is there any propriety in the objection, that, if it be necessary to conform baptism to circumcision, women ought not to be baptized. For, if it be evident that the sign of circumcision testified the sanctification of the seed of Israel, there can be no doubt that it was given equally for the sanctification of males and females. And though only the males were circumcised, ... the females were in a certain sense partakers of their circumcision,"* To this may be added another suggestion, which the writer has never heard offered, nor ever seen in print, but which has afforded to his own mind an easy and natural solution of

* Calv. Inst. vol. 2, bk. iv., chap. xvi.

this apparent difficulty. Repeated reference has already been made to the proselyte baptism of the Jews, which had come to be appended to the rite of circumcision, in the case of pagan converts. What improbability is there in concluding that pagan females as well as males received this baptism when they became Jews; and that when Christ exalted this ceremony, by making it an initiatory ordinance for his Church, in place of that bloody rite to which it was an unauthorized appendage, women and men alike continued to be baptized? And the same idea carried out would give confirmation to the doctrine of infant baptism, since it is altogether probable that the entire households of these pagan converts to Judaism were baptized, as well as all the males circumcised. From all this, therefore, it may be argued, that the apostles would naturally take the command of our Lord to baptize the nations to signify that they should baptize by *households* those nations which they discipled, administering the rite to the children of the converts equally as to the converts themselves, and thereby receiving entire families to the bosom of the Church. And the probability that such would be their understanding of our Lord's command is greatly increased by the fact (to which your attention has already been called) that the complete course of instruction, even of adults, in the Christian doctrines was to be imparted *after* baptism—not before it—which brings out, also, most beautifully the idea of the systematic teaching and culture which the Church is bound to impart to her infant members during their Christian minority.

Turning our consideration now from the commission itself to the recorded practice of the apostles in fulfilling this commission, we shall find that the actual interpretation by them of the command to disciple the nations was precisely that which we have just marked out as the only probable interpretation. On the day of Pentecost, at the very first Christian baptism, Peter invited his hearers to the reception of the ordinance in the following language: "Repent, and be baptized every one of you in the name of Jesus Christ for the remission of sins, and ye shall receive the gift of the Holy Ghost. *For the promise is unto you and to your children.** We are aware that some commentators consider this declaration as denoting merely, in a general sense, that the promises of God would descend upon the posterity of believers for generations to come. But, taken in its connection, it seems hardly possible that the application of the passage should not be more specific than this view makes it. We agree rather with the following paraphrase and explanation of it, from the pen of Matthew Henry: "Your children shall still have, as they have had, an interest in the

* Acts ii. 38, 39.

covenant, and a title to the external seal of it. Come over to Christ, to receive those inestimable benefits; for the promise of the remission of sins, and the gift of the Holy Ghost, is to you and to your children. When God took Abraham into covenant, he said, 'I will be a God unto thee and to thy seed,'* and accordingly every Israelite had his son circumcised at eight days old. Now it is proper for an Israelite, when he is by baptism to come into a new dispensation of this covenant, to ask, ' What must be done with my children? Must they be thrown out, or taken with me?' 'Taken in,' says Peter, ' by all means; for the promise, that great promise of God's being to you a God, is as much to you *and to your children* now as ever it was." And when it is stated, a little further on in the narrative, that " the same day there were added unto them about three thousand souls," the more probable supposition is, that in this three thousand

* Gen. xvii. 7.

were included all ages, *infant children* as well as men and women.

Again, in Acts xvi. 14, 15, we are told that "Lydia, a seller of purple of the city of Thyatira, ... whose heart the Lord opened, that she attended unto the things that were spoken of Paul, ... was baptized, *and her household.*" In the same chapter, verse 33d, we have an account of another family baptism. This is the family of the Philippian jailer, who was converted at midnight, and was immediately "baptized, he and *all his*," says the sacred record. And in 1 Cor. i. 16, St. Paul tells us that he "baptized the *household* of Stephanas." Now these three families must have constituted a miraculous exception to the ordinary range of households if there were no infant children in any of them. But if the membership of these three families included one single child not yet arrived at years of discretion, then the baptism of that child is definitely affirmed, our argument is incontrovertibly sustained, and the fact is established that the apostles understood the commission to baptize all nations as embracing in its design infants as well as adults. We contend that the probabilities here are so strong as to amount almost to a demonstration in favor of infant baptism. And since nothing whatever can be found in the Bible (either in the Old or New Testament) to contradict the conclusion here drawn, or to forbid the administering of the ordinance to infants, we might with propriety rest our proof here, under the sure conviction that it is immovable.

But before dismissing the subject, some of the most prominent objections urged against the doctrine of infant baptism will be considered and answered. And,

1. It is said, that the argument we adduce from circumcision is good for nothing, since that ceremony was a national rite only, and not a church ordinance; since

the person circumcised was thereby admitted indeed into citizenship in the Jewish nation, but not into membership in the Jewish Church.

We answer, it was *both* a national rite and a church ordinance. We claim, that its highest and most important signification had reference to things spiritual. And here again we might rightfully throw the burden of proof on the other side, by asking, Was there no visible Church prior to Christ's coming? And if there were, did it exist without any ordinances? What was its initiatory ordinance, if circumcision was not? Our design, however, is not merely to baffle, but to convince. Therefore we will cite the 38th verse of the 7th chapter of Acts, where the Israelitish camp at Sinai is expressly denominated "*the Church* in the wilderness."

2. It is argued, that faith is requisite to a membership in Christ's Church; that infants cannot exercise faith, and there-

fore cannot properly be admitted to the Church.

This objection, if it proves anything, proves quite too much. Faith is requisite to salvation. But will any of our objectors hold that infants cannot be saved because they cannot believe? In the face of the declaration of our Saviour, "Of such is the kingdom of heaven," will they contend that all who die in infancy perish? But none are saved who do not belong to the Church invisible, who are not effectually redeemed by Christ's atonement, and regenerated by his Spirit. If then they are worthy to belong to the invisible Church, and to experience the regenerating power of the Holy Ghost, are they not fit also for a membership in the visible Church, and may not the baptismal sign and seal of regeneration be applied to their foreheads?

But again, faith was a requisite under the Old Testament economy no less than under the New. Read the account of that long list of worthies contained in the 11th chapter of the Epistle to the Hebrews, and then notice at its close the declaration, "these all having obtained a good report *through faith.*" And what saith Paul in Rom. ii. 28, 29?—" He is not a Jew, which is one outwardly; neither is that circumcision, which is outward in the flesh: but he is a Jew, which is one inwardly; and circumcision is that of the heart, in the spirit, and not in the letter; whose praise is not of men, but of God."

Again, Gal. iii. 9, 29: "So then they which be of faith are blessed with faithful Abraham. And if ye be Christ's, then are ye Abraham's seed, and heirs according to the promise." And again, Rom. iv. 11: "He"—that is, Abraham—"received the sign of circumcision, a seal of the righteousness of the faith which he had yet being uncircumcised: that he might be the father of all them that believe." And once more, Rom. xv. 8: "Jesus Christ was a minister of the circumcision for the truth of God, to confirm the promises made unto the fathers."

How could there possibly be fabricated a stronger chain of proof than these passages afford, that in the Abrahamic Church, equally as in the Christian, faith was required for membership, and that the initiatory ordinance of the Church, then as now, was the sign and seal of this faith? Yet we know that this ordinance (circumcision) was administered to infants as well as to adults, and that this was done by God's appointment. Hence the objection against infant baptism which we are now considering falls to the ground.

3. It is objected, that all Church members have a right to partake of both its sacraments; and that consistency would require us, who recognize infants as members, to bring them with us to the sacrament of the Lord's Supper.

Our answer is, We deny the premise,

that all Church members are of right entitled to partake of both the Church sacraments. There may be members of the Church who are not and ought not to be members in full communion. It is indeed no unfrequent thing (though we are sorry to be compelled to admit it) that an adult member of the Church is forbidden by the church officers to come to the Lord's table, on account of something in his life manifestly inconsistent with the Christian character; nor is he restored to full communion until he exhibits due repentance; yet, while under censure, he is still acknowledged as a church member. It may happen, also, that from an inward consciousness of lack of faith, or because of some other real or imagined disqualification, a truly worthy member may for a time refrain voluntarily from partaking of this sacrament;—often, indeed, much to his spiritual detriment, but not to the loss of his membership, unless too long persisted in. Now, nothing but open inconsistency or such conscious unworthiness should prevent the baptized child from coming forward to this ordinance so soon as he can come understandingly. Up to the time of his attaining a suitable age, he is *naturally* disqualified, and is in the same position in which the infant Hebrew stood with regard to the passover. If the latter, therefore, could be a member of the " Church in the wilderness," although for a time physically incapacitated to be a sharer in one of her sacraments, why may not the former be a member of the Christian Church, although for a season under the same physical incapacity?

An apt illustration of the same principle may be found in secular affairs, in the status which *native-born minors* hold in this country. They are citizens of the United States, as really and truly such as they will be when of full age, and yet they are restrained from exercising one of the most prominent and most highly valued rights of citizenship, not being allowed to vote until they are twenty-one years of age.

4. Another objection urged is, that it is unjust to place the seal of church-membership upon an unconscious infant; and to make solemn vows for that infant, binding him to their fulfillment.

It is a sufficient answer to this objection to say that God is the author of the arrangement; and man is in no way responsible for its justice or its injustice. The objectors, therefore, are in this plea calling in question God's justice and not man's, and they may well be left to settle the matter with the infinitely wise and holy Being whom they thus offend. It may be observed, however, in passing, that the acting of the parent for the child in this matter is by no means an isolated and exceptional case. Not only do we find many instances recorded in the Bible where the actions of parents have, under God's appointment, brought obligations or imposed penalties upon their infant offspring; but, in the workings of God's providence around us, and in the every-day affairs of life as regulated by men themselves, we see and approve of the same principle, exhibited in manifold ways.

Who will dispute the fact, that the children of Hindoo or of African parents are *born pagans*, and inherit all the disadvantages of their unfortunate birth, and that, too, without any fault of their own? Who will deny that children born in England or the United States are by birth, and independent of any volition on their part, either American or English citizens, and as such entitled to all the political, social, and religious privileges conferred by such a citizenship, and subject also to a citizen's obligations and duties? Still further, is not this citizenship of the child oftentimes changed, while the child is yet too young to entertain an opinion or to have a voice respecting the matter, by the voluntary act of the parent, when that parent adopts a new country as his home, and takes the oath of allegiance to the government of that country?

And just so is it, by God's appointment, with reference to the Church, and its privileges and obligations. The children of non-professors hold the same position as their parents, and are to be accounted as outside the pale of the Church, until by their own act they become, as it were, naturalized, and obtain a citizenship within it:—while the children of professing Christians are by virtue of their birth " fellow-citizens with the saints," and members of the visible Church. Hence, the seal of such membership is their birth-right, and to withhold it from them is to rob them of their rightful inheritance. Hence, also, they are solemnly bound to perform all the duties of such an inherited membership, as advancing years and knowledge render these duties apparent. And the same holds true of a child, only one of whose parents has made a public profession of faith in Christ; for, as St. Paul explains it in 1 Cor. vii. 14, "The unbelieving husband is sanctified by the wife, and the unbelieving wife is sanctified by the husband; else were your children unclean, but now are they holy."

5. The last objection which appears to us of sufficient importance to claim attention is, that the tendency of such teaching and such practice as we adopt in regard to infants is to lower the standard of personal piety in the Church, by introducing into it many whose hearts have not been truly wrought upon by the Holy Ghost, but who, having received the sign and seal of church membership while yet unconscious, grow up without feeling the obligations thus laid upon them, and often assume the full vows of Christianity as a form only, without having experienced any real change of heart, or at all having felt the regenerating and sanctifying power of Divine grace.

To this objection our main answer must be, "Who art thou, O man, that repliest against God?" God's wisdom is perfect, even though it often goes counter to our feeble judgments. And if we are clearly directed by his inspired word to a certain line of conduct which appears injudicious or unwise to us, that affords no reason for an abandonment of the course marked out; but it should urge us to a more careful study of the exact directions given, and to a more earnest caution lest some failure on our part shall be the fruitful cause of miscarriage in the scheme. God's power is not limited, any more than his wisdom is imperfect. If Christian parents as individuals, and the Church as a whole, and the pastors as overseers of the flock, would perform all their duty toward the tender lambs of the fold, there would not so many of them go astray upon the mountains of folly, or become hopelessly lost in the tangled mazes of sin's wilderness.

The highest state of the Church, that to which God means she shall eventually be brought, and to which she would speedily attain were all her members strong in the faith—the state of her millennial glory—will undoubtedly show the sublime spectacle of race after race of children and of children's children, *all* growing up in the fear and favor of God, *all* walking in the commandments and ordinances of the Lord blameless, *all* from early infancy placing implicit trust in Christ as their Saviour, *all* in mature years reflecting his purity in their daily lives. And this will be, not because the moral natures of the infant offspring will be any less susceptible of evil than now, not because they will any the less need the regeneration of the Holy Ghost; but it will be because the Church shall then "arise and shine, her light being come," and "God shall be in the midst of her," and that to bless; it will be because God's people will be faithful on their part in caring for their offspring, and therefore, God, who is always faithful on his part, will attest the truth of his promise, "I will be a God unto thee and to thy seed after thee."*

Solomon has said, "Train up a child in the way he should go: and when he is old, he will not depart from it."† This assertion we recognize as the truthful utterance of inspiration, and we regard it as declaring not merely that the aged sinner will at last remember the religious training of his early years, and become obedient to the long-forgotten and despised lessons of his childhood, but rather that all the way along from infancy to old age those who are properly trained up in the right way will be so kept as not to depart from this way. And whenever we see a child going astray from the paths of holiness, we feel assured that there has been some error in the training of that child. In other words, we fully believe that a perfect Christian training

* Gen. xvii. 7. † Prov. xxii. 6.

would be certain to result in a Christian child.

And this, not at all because we think that the parent or any other human agency has power to renew the heart of the child; nor because we in the least give place to that unscriptural theory, that the mind of an infant is like a sheet of blank paper, to be written upon at will—possessed of no moral character, and as ready to choose holiness as sin. By no means. Sin is the polluting curse of our whole race; and a sinful nature, the terrible inheritance of every new-born child. But we hold fast to God's promises: "Yea, let God be true, but every man a liar."* The promises of Jehovah are to us *and to our children;* and if there is no failure on our part, these promises will prove as true in regard to our offspring as in regard to ourselves.†

* Rom. iii. 4.

† The same principle, for which we here contend in spiritual things, was often illustrated in temporal things during the earthly sojourn of Jesus, by the physical cures which he

Regeneration is often at so early a period that the time of the change is entirely unknown to the subject of it. This has been the case with some of the most eminent saints that have ever lived. They began to love Jesus so early that they could remember no time when their hearts were not in loving sympathy with their Saviour. And why may not this be the case usually, instead of being a rare exception? A recent writer* says with no less pertinence than truth: "There are three parties to this covenant sealed in the baptism of children—God, the parent and the child. Originally, the first two are the responsible stipulators. At the age of majority the child comes in the place of the parent. God will be faithful. If the other parties fulfill the conditions, he will convey the covenanted

wrought upon children because of their parents' faith; see Matt. xv. 22, et seq.; Mark ix. 14, et seq.; and, also, by the cure of a servant because of his master's faith; Matt. viii. 5, et seq.

* In the Biblical Repertory of Jan., 1857, pp. 24 and 25.

blessings. If they are not conveyed, the fault is *with them*, one or both."

And in this connection, the government of children must not be lost sight of. Certain it is, that the proper government must be united with all our other training, in order to success. God must be able to say of us, as he said of faithful Abraham, " I know him, that he will command his children and his household after him, and they shall keep the way of the Lord, to do justice and judgment; that the Lord may bring upon Abraham that which he hath spoken of him."* We must have also boldness of faith, to say as did Joshua, " As for me *and my house*, we will serve the Lord."† But, withal, we must remember that it is quite as easy to err and fail by governing too much, as by not governing enough. We must pray daily for wisdom to guide us in the discharge of this great duty, and for grace to take the blame

---

* Gen. xviii. 19.   † Josh. xxiv. 15.

to ourselves, if our children should fail to be converted, instead of imputing anything to God's failure as regards his covenant promises.

But, besides the failure of parents to do their full duty to their children, the pastors of churches and church sessions have been guilty of dereliction in not taking a proper oversight of the baptized children. The injunction of Christ, " Feed my lambs," has not been sufficiently regarded. The whole Church has been guilty together in this matter. Instead of viewing these lambs as really a part of the flock, and sheltering them securely within the fold, and there feeding and nourishing them according to their tender years, too frequently have they cruelly shut them out of the safe enclosure where the flock is gathered, and thus left them, as it were, a ready prey to wild beasts.

The children of the Church too often have not been viewed, or been taught to view themselves, as being born into any special relation to the people of God, or as under any specially solemn obligation to love the Saviour, and to live as becometh godliness. But they have been in practice, if not in theory, ranked in the same category as the unbaptized children of non-professors; and the birth-right of membership in the Church as children of the faithful has been lost sight of, if not absolutely disowned.

Two great and sore evils have sprung from this failure of the Church to comprehend and to believe the covenant promises of Jehovah concerning the children of the Church. One is, that many conversions have been prevented, which would have taken place in early infancy had the Church been properly imbued with faith; for it is true in behalf of our offspring, no less than in behalf of ourselves, that *according to our faith* it is done to us. Blessings are only promised to the believing. What wonder, then, if we will not believe God's promises, that he should refrain from blessing us?

The other evil is, that the spiritual treatment of baptized children, after they have arrived at years of discretion, has been oftentimes exceedingly unwise, and in cases not a few positively pernicious. Ignoring God's solemn covenant concerning them, and hence assuming, as a matter of course, that their hearts have remained unrenewed during the period of infancy, the efforts put forth for their spiritual welfare have all been direct efforts at conversion, based upon the foregone conclusion that they are still at enmity with God, and abiding under his wrath; whereas,. a judicious examination into their spiritual state would not unfrequently have revealed the fact of their already effected regeneration, and would have furnished convincing proof to the children themselves, as well as to those who had the spiritual oversight of them, of their true love to God, and their sincere desire and purpose to serve him. Where such is the case, all that is requisite to the complete development on their part of a consistent Christian character is the proper guidance of their young minds to a correct understanding of Christian doctrine, and to a clear perception of Christian duty. When the right way is made known to them, they will be found willing and rejoiced to walk in it. And wherein such young Christians err, their errors will be the errors of childish impulse, or of youthful indiscretion, rather than of cherished wicked intent (errors far less inconsistent with, or damaging to, the Christian character than many which we witness and bear with in adult disciples); and kindly admonition and rebuke will seldom be lost upon them.

But, for want of such a judicious eliciting and cultivation of the grace of God that is in them, doubtless many have been left to walk all their lifetime in spiritual darkness, who were nevertheless regenerate almost from birth, and who might have been rendered bright and shining lights in Zion. By reason, also, of the misjudged efforts for their conversion to which I have alluded, many have been sorely perplexed and troubled; because, when dealt with as impenitent sinners and haters of God, this theoretical assumption as to their spiritual condition has been so totally antagonistic to their own actual experience, which has, from their earliest years, been in truth a Christian experience.

Let us be careful not to exclude our children from any precious privilege which is theirs by birth-right, or to cast any stumbling-block in the way of their Christian enjoyment and usefulness. Let us rise to the perfect comprehension of God's promises concerning our offspring, in order that our faith may seize for them the covenant blessings.

Sacrament of the Lord's Supper.

" This do in remembrance of me."—LUKE xxii. 19.

" Take, eat: this is my body, which is broken for you: this do in remembrance of me. . . . This cup is the new testament in my blood: this do ye, as oft as ye drink it, in remembrance of me. For as often as ye eat this bread, and drink this cup, ye do show the Lord's death till he come."—I COR. xi. 24, 25, 26.

" The cup of blessing which we bless, is it not the communion of the blood of Christ? The bread which we break, is it not the communion of the body of Christ?" I COR. x. 16.

CHAPTER IV.

Sacrament of the Lord's Supper.

THE Design of this Sacrament.—Early Church practices with respect to the ordinance.—Historical development of doctrinal errors concerning it.—Scriptural refutation of these errors.—Who are proper participants of the ordinance?—The effect of partaking—upon those who partake unworthily—upon worthy participants.

THIS sacrament was instituted by our blessed Lord as a *new memorial rite* for his Church, to succeed the long-observed festival of the passover. "This do in *remembrance* of me," were his words at its institution.

God has a perfect understanding of the mechanism of the human mind; and he knows full well that man is prone to forget. The most vivid impressions soon fade from the memory unless there is something to remind us of them.

You may look upon a smiling landscape, wondrous in its beauty, with its flowery mead and its winding stream, its waving forests and its rugged heights, its pastures of bleating flocks, and its fields of golden grain and the whole gemmed with dew-drops, sparkling like diamond-points in the first rays of the morning sun; and you may think that the glowing reality can never be effaced from your memory. But let nothing call up that scene to your mind—speak of it to no friend—write it in no journal—pencil it upon no canvas—and in a very few brief years the outline will grow dim upon the brain; and if by chance it should again be called to remembrance, you will wonder at your former admiration of the scene; for now the mountain will seem to be confounded with the meadow, the pearly stream will be indistinct and muddy in its windings, grain, grove and grazing herd will appear mingled together in inextricable confusion, the morning dew will have become a thick mist to obscure the whole, and there will be no longer in the changed scene, presented by your faltering memory, aught to delight or to attract.

Let your best loved and your most intimate friend die, and, though you be allowed to possess no painting or daguerreotype of him, his features will for a while remain so impressed upon your memory that you will in imagination see him before you wherever you look with all the distinctness and reality of actual life. But time will do its work; and one by one those well-known features will fade from your remembrance, until at last, with the utmost stretch and tension of your mind, you will be unable vividly to recall them.

Hence it is, that there is a great advantage in having, and indeed an almost absolute necessity to have, some reminder or memorial of what we would sacredly cherish in our memories. And for this reason, the Lord Jesus, when about to leave the earth, prepared a memorial for his Church of that which he wished them above all things to keep in mind.

Again, our memory is still more treacherous than it would otherwise be, from the fact that things present are continually jostling us, and claiming all our attention and all our thought, so that there is little or no opportunity for our minds to go out spontaneously after things bygone or absent. We need something, therefore, to break the spell of this complete absorption with the present; to interrupt the perpetual current of excitement which springs from present cares and present duties and present enjoyments; and to turn our minds backward, to the contemplation of those things which ought to be remembered. but which are in danger of being wholly and for ever forgotten. For this reason, also, the departing Saviour instituted a perpetual memorial for his Church.

And besides, he knew that such remembrance would confer gratification. It is a pleasant thing to be able to call up vividly before our minds those persons and those events that are dear to us. Hence, it is pleasant to have in our possession something which shall excite and strengthen our memory in regard to them, and which shall turn us from the all-engrossing events of to-day to their contemplation. And in this happiness, which he knew it would afford his believing followers to the end of time, we have a third reason why Christ instituted such a memorial rite.

Thus, the natural proneness of the human mind to forget, the distraction of memory by the constant pressure of surrounding circumstances, and the delight afforded by the possession of loved objects, all argue the wisdom of Christ in establishing the sacrament of the Lord's Supper as an ordinance of remembrance to his Church for all ages.

Again, this ordinance is a memorial of *Christ.* "This do in remembrance of *me.*"

And it is not a little striking and significant, that the only memorial ordinance established by the Lord Jesus for his Church was one to keep *himself* in remembrance. In this way, he has presented himself before us as the highest possible object upon which our memory can fasten.

If we forget all things else, Christ must not be forgotten. He is the Sun of our moral firmament—the "Sun of righteousness," that rose upon our night of sin "with healing in his wings." Obscure his rays, and moral darkness, impenetrable, hopeless, will again settle over the earth. And as with the race, so also with every individual of the race. Every sinner who is enlightened is enlightened by his beams; and when he is obliterated from the memory, the soul sinks back again irrevocably into the night of sin.

He is the centre of all Church history. To him point all the types of the old dispensation; and around him cluster all the symbols of the new. Of him spake the ancient prophets, who in rapt visions beheld his coming glory; and concerning him discoursed the apostles, who caught their eloquence from his lips, and received their inspiration from the baptism of his Spirit. To his praises were turned the choicest melodies of the Hebrew poets, and in celebration of his honors heaven's high arches echo to the sound of angelic anthems. Who would not like a memorial of him who is the object of the admiring reverence of the entire universe of holy beings? And in this sacrament such a memorial is left us.

But, more specifically, this memorial points to the *death* of Christ. Its design was to commemorate the fact and the manner of his suffering death for the sins of the world. To this accord the significant emblems used in the ordinance; and also the added words of Paul in 1 Cor. xi. 26: "For as often as ye eat this bread, and drink this cup, ye do show the Lord's death till he come."

Christ's death was the crowning act of the whole scheme of redemption. It was not enough, that he should humble himself to dwell with sinners in human form. It was not enough, that he should keep inviolate the holy law of God, and thus do honor to those precepts which the whole human race had broken. It was not enough, that, in his character as man, he should live a perfectly sinless life, and thus prove that there is nothing in our natures incompatible with God's strict demands for obedience—nothing in our bodies or our souls necessarily at war with holiness, except as they have been brought under the power of sin. It was not enough, that he should pass through all the discomforts, the trials and sufferings of earth, in order to be able to sympathize fully in every sorrow of earth's children. It was not enough, that he should be subjected to the fiercest, as well as the most subtle and crafty, assaults of the devil, that he might know how to succor those who are tempted. It was not enough, even, that he should feel the burden of a world's sin laid on his shoulders, when praying in the garden—so weighty as to exhaust his strength, and to require an angel to be sent from heaven as his supporter—so terribly oppressive to his pure soul as to convulse him with agony, causing the great drops of blood-like sweat to fall from his brow, and drawing forth that earnest prayer, "O my Father, if it be possible, let this cup pass from me."*

No, no, he must drink the bitter cup even to the very dregs! He must feel upon the cross, for a few terrible moments, that all the Father's fond affection for him, as the

* Matt. xxvi. 39.

only begotten Son of his love, is veiled behind a cloud of anger that is ready to burst upon him as the representative of transgressors! He must even bear the shock of the bursting cloud, and must expire under it, with an awful realization of the fact, that when he stands in the sinner's place, to receive the sinner's punishment, he must expect to be "forsaken" of his Father! Yes, it was only by his *death* that the great work of atonement could be completed, and a sufficient satisfaction be rendered to God's violated law to enable him to be "just" and, at the same time, "the justifier of him which believeth in Jesus."* This ordinance was instituted, therefore, in order that it might commemorate the great event which perfected our purchase-price, and rendered it possible for us to be saved.

Nor is the fact that this ordinance is designed to keep in perpetual remembrance

* Rom. iii. 26.

the death of our Saviour at all antagonistic to what our Church standards teach concerning the sacraments, as laid down in the introductory chapter. For, while the two sacraments differ in this, that baptism is designed as an initiatory ordinance, to be administered once for all at the reception of a member to the visible Church, but the Lord's Supper as a memorial ordinance, to be often repeated in the assemblies of the faithful; yet it is true that in each alike, "Christ and the benefits of the new covenant are represented, sealed and applied to believers."

All "the benefits of the new covenant" rest upon the sacrificial death of Christ, and hence it is only necessary to show that Christ's death is represented in this ordinance, and that the benefits flowing from his death are sealed and applied to believers. That his death is represented in it will at once appear, from the very fact that it was instituted with the specific design of

commemorating his death. That the benefits flowing from his death are, in it, sealed and applied to believers, is proved by the experience of every Christian who, with faith, receives the emblems of the broken bread and the poured-out wine: for, whenever he does this, the Holy Spirit witnesses with his spirit that he is obeying the injunction of his Divine Master, not in its letter merely, but according to its deeper spiritual import; and thus his conscience is stamped anew with the seal of God's approbation. Also, as he partakes of the visible emblems, the crucified Saviour is presented more palpably before him as the true object of faith; and thereby his faith is quickened, and he is enabled to feed spiritually upon the body and blood of Jesus Christ, and to experience for himself what the Saviour meant when he said, " My flesh is meat indeed, and my blood is drink indeed."*
The Holy Spirit is always present in the

* John vi. 55.

ordinance, to apply to believing participants the benefits of that sacred mystery which is symbolized, and to bless those who eat with proper discernment of the Lord's body.

In the further treatment of this subject, the plan will be to mention the practices of the early Church in relation to the Lord's Supper, and to trace the historical development of several erroneous doctrines concerning it; then to discuss these errors, showing their antagonism to the word of God; and lastly, to answer the inquiries, Who may properly partake of this ordinance? and, What is its effect upon those who do partake of it?

Commencing with the Apostolic Church immediately after the resurrection of our Saviour, we find several incidental proofs in the New Testament that the custom of Christians then was, to celebrate this ordinance very frequently, perhaps as often as they met in public or social religious assemblies. Thus, in Acts xx. 7, the first day of the week is spoken of as the time when the disciples " came together to break bread," by which is undoubtedly meant the partaking of the Lord's Supper: and a number of the most learned and accurate commentators are of opinion that the same interpretation is to be put upon Acts ii. 46, where we are told that those who had gladly received the word on the day of Pentecost continued *daily* in " the breaking of bread from house to house." An able modern German writer, in commenting on this passage, remarks as follows: " The ancient Christians were in the habit of eating together daily, or holding the love-feast, and never took a common meal without observing the Lord's Supper. In the Apostolic Church at Jerusalem there appears to have obtained, as is plain from the very idea of a community of goods, a family union of all believers in the strictest and most proper sense. Accordingly, they took food together daily, that is, they celebrated the ('agapæ') love-feast, and to the common meal the Lord's Supper likewise was appended."* If this be the correct view of the passage (and a careful examination of it would seem to uphold the opinion), then this ordinance was *daily* celebrated during that precious season of ingathering which began with Pentecost; and, as we have already seen, continued to be observed in the Apostolic Church at least as often as once a week, or upon every recurring Lord's day.

The custom just referred to, of appending the Lord's Supper to a love-feast, or meal enjoyed by the rich and poor together in common, was in imitation of its first institution by Christ, which took place at the close of the paschal feast; although there is nothing in the instructions of our Lord, when he instituted this ordinance, which at all sanctions such a custom; and it is evi-

* Ols. Com. on Acts ii. 46.

dent that he designed it as a substitution for the passover, to be observed by Christians in place of that feast, and not as an appendage to it, or to any other meal. Nor is it probable that the apostles and their associates had any idea of making the preceding meal at all an essential part of the proper celebration of the ordinance; but only that while the number of disciples was still limited, and while, from the peculiar circumstances of persecution and of trial attending the first planting of Christianity, these disciples were necessarily led to a community of interest in pecuniary affairs, and to a peculiar intimacy of association in social life, it was found more convenient, and at least equally appropriate, thus to celebrate the Lord's death together at the close of an ordinary meal, partaken of in common.

But, what was thus at first a natural, though by no means an obligatory, practice, soon came to be regarded as an essential; and, when so regarded and practiced, opened the way for the letting in of many evils. Soon this preceding meal, which was at first very simple, and made up of the joint contributions of all who partook of it, became a sumptuous entertainment, attended with unchristian distinctions as to the places assigned and the treatment shown to the richer and to the poorer guests. Thus the minds of all were unfitted for a proper reception of those emblems which symbolized the holy mystery of Christ's death, and jealousies and heart-burnings were caused by the preferences of persons practiced.

Especially rapid was this tendency in developing itself among the proselytes from heathenism, accustomed as they had been previously to pagan festivals in honor of their gods, at which the most immoderate excesses were allowed. Accordingly we find that in the Church at Corinth, even in the Apostolic age, the evils alluded to had become so glaring as to call for a special rebuke from St. Paul, who had founded that Church. He tells them plainly, that what they did at the close of such an unbrotherly and riotous feast, in which "every one took before other his own supper," and where "one was hungry and another drunken,"* was by no means the celebration of that simple memorial festival which Christ instituted; for, though they might partake of the bread and the wine as directed, they could not truly eat the Lord's Supper under such circumstances. "What!" he exclaims, "have ye not houses to eat and to drink in? Or, despise ye the Church of God, and shame them that have not?" Then, in order the more effectually to correct these abuses, he states clearly what pertains to a proper observance of this ordinance; cautions them against the danger of an unworthy participation in it; and concludes with an injunction to satisfy their hunger at home, and

* 1 Cor. xi. 21.

thus to separate the eating of the Lord's Supper from all thought of mere bodily nourishment or sensual gratification, in order that they might truly discern in it the Lord's body, and receive from it the highest spiritual benefit.

This severe censure of the Corinthian Church by the Apostle Paul doubtless had the effect of correcting for a time the evils that had arisen from appending the Lord's Supper to a common meal, although the love-feast still continued to be observed precedent to the other and more sacred ordinance.

But the evil tendencies of this unauthorized joining of things common and sacred afterward developed themselves anew, and to a more alarming extent; so that before the close of the fourth century of the Christian era, the abuse of the love-feasts had become too notorious to be longer tolerated, and "in the year 397 A. D., the Council of Carthage ordained that they should not be held in the churches except in cases of particular necessity."* From about this period the celebration of the Lord's Supper appears to have been disjoined from the agapæ, or love-feast, and united with other parts of divine service;† and the love-feast, either at once or gradually, to have been discontinued. The observance of the Lord's Supper, however, was still held to constitute an essential part of the worship of every Sunday; and the whole church partook of it, after joining in the Amen of the preceding prayer.

In its celebration at this period, Neander tells us that " The deacons carried the bread and wine to every one present in order." The custom of surrounding a table as at a meal had apparently been discontinued with the love-feasts, and the custom of kneeling to receive the elements had not yet sprung up. But, the same

* Rel. Encyclop., Art. "Agapæ."
† Nean. Hist., vol. i. p. 327.

historian further tells us, that it was now "held to be necessary that all the Christians in the place should, by participating in this communion, maintain their union with the Lord and with his Church; hence the deacons carried a portion of the consecrated bread and wine to strangers, to the sick, to prisoners and to all who were prevented from being present at the assembly."* This fact is deserving of careful notice, since in it we may discern the first buddings of an undue exaltation of the material elements used at the Supper, as if they contained in themselves a mystical power, an inherent "principle of imperishable life," and were capable of communicating a "magical advantage," independent of the disposition of the heart."†

The penetrating mind of Origen, who lived previous to this period,‡ had already

* Nean. Hist., vol. i. p. 332.
† Ibid., vol. i. pp. 648, 649.
‡ Died A. D. 253.

discovered the beginning of such an erroneous notion in his day, and had earnestly combated it. "We neither lose anything," he says, "by failing to partake of the consecrated bread by itself considered; nor do we gain anything by the bare partaking of that bread; but the reason why one man has less, and another more, is the good or bad disposition of each individual. The earthly bread is by itself in no respect different from any other food."*

This superstitious regard for the consecrated elements rapidly increased; and not long afterward we find that a portion of the consecrated bread was borne away from the sacramental supper by many of the communicants, and partaken of by them every day before engaging in any worldly employment. Others took it with them in sea-voyages, that they might always have it in their power to partake of the sacrament by the way.

* Nean. Hist., vol. i. p. 649.

Another step in this begun path of superstition was soon taken, and pieces of the bread that had been consecrated were bound upon the person, under the impression that they would act as a potent charm to preserve from shipwreck and from other calamities. Thus a brother of Ambrose,* one of the fathers of the fourth century, attributed his rescue from a wrecked ship to the wonderful virtue of an amulet of consecrated bread, which he had obtained from a church member, although he was himself as yet unbaptized.†

This superstition was also the occasion of a most fatal departure from the original form of institution of this sacrament. The same undue exaltation of the elements which ascribed such mystic power to the bread, prevented from carrying away any of the consecrated wine, lest sacrilege should be committed by spilling it; and

* Ambrose died A. D. 397. (Anthon's Class. Dict.)
† Nean. Hist., vol. ii. p. 329.

hence, those who communicated in private partook of the bread only. This is the germ of that unauthorized withholding of the cup from the laity, which, some centuries later, was developed into an established doctrine of the Papal Church.

Thus there came to be that reverent regard for the material elements employed in this ordinance, which belonged of right only to the crucified Jesus, whose death the elements symbolized. "The bread and wine were now everywhere *elevated* before distribution, so that they might be seen by the people, and be viewed with reverence; and hence arose, not long after, the *adoration of the symbols*."*

The ordinance was now gradually coming to be regarded as *in itself a sacrifice*, instead of the symbolical representation of a sacrifice. This erroneous conception had not yet, indeed, taken a definite form. It required several centuries more of progres-

* Mosh. Eccl. Hist., vol. i. p. 281.

sive departure from the simplicity of the gospel, to give it tangible shape, and to unfold it in all its practically pernicious workings. But the baneful seed had been sown, and had already sprung up, which was subsequently developed into a mature growth.

Naturally, the inquiry arose, what imparted to the bread and the wine that magical power which, as we have seen, they were supposed to possess after consecration? And with equal naturalness, this power was attributed to the actual presence of Christ in these elements. Thus, stating wrongly, by investing the symbol with a potency which belonged only to that which it represented, they were driven necessarily to the only logical, and yet the fallacious conclusion, that what was symbolized had taken actual possession of the symbol, and was in reality at all times present in it. Hence, in order to consistency, they were forced to endorse this plain, logical deduction from their first error, and to advance the false doctrine that Jesus was in very deed actually present in the bread and in the wine from the moment of consecration. *How* this real presence was brought about was for a long time a point of controversy, until one *Paschasius Radbert*, monk and afterward abbot of Corbey, in A. D. 831, took the bold ground, "that by virtue of the consecration, by a miracle of Almighty power, the substance of the bread and wine became converted into the substance of the body and blood of Christ, so that beneath the sensible outward emblems of the bread and wine, another substance was still present." "If thou believest," he says, "in the miracle of the incarnation of the Son of God, thou must believe also in the miracle which is wrought by the same divine power through the words of the priest. The *same body* is here present as that in which Christ was born, suffered, arose and ascended to heaven. Simply to avoid any shock to the senses, while an opportunity is furnished for the exercise of faith, the miracle is performed after a hidden manner, discernible only to faith, under the still subsisting outward forms of color, taste and touch."* And he asserts also (and cites pretended instances to prove it), that to satisfy the earnest longings of individuals, and to remove doubts, the body and blood of Christ have been sometimes perceptibly presented to the sight; although, at their distribution by the priest, they resumed their previous covering, and appeared again as bread and wine.

The Church, corrupt as it had then become, was not yet prepared to give its authoritative sanction to so bold a statement of this new doctrine. But, in the Lateran Council, "A. D. 1215, Pope Innocent III., a most imperious pontiff, without asking the opinion of any one, published seventy decrees," and among other things declared

* Nean. Ch. Hist., vol. iii. p. 495.

that such is the true doctrine concerning the sacrament of the Lord's Supper. To this doctrine he gave the "hitherto unknown term of *transubstantiation.*"* Such is the belief on this subject now universally entertained by the Romish Church, and such the name by which it is designated.

The evil growth was at last matured. The symbol had fully usurped the place of that which it symbolized. The sacramental ordinance was no longer an emblem of Christ's death; it was, at every repetition, the literal dying anew of Christ. Its constant celebration, therefore, kept up a perpetual sacrifice of the Son of God. His body was perpetually broken afresh, and mangled in the eating. His blood was made perpetually to flow in the poured-out wine. According to this view, the priesthood, instead of being done away in Christ, as we believe it was, must needs be continued. So long as sacrifices are to be per-

* Mosh. Eccl. Hist., vol. ii. p. 334.

formed, there must be priests to officiate at the altar.

The doctrine of "Transubstantiation" opens the way also for another most pernicious error. The Romish view of the real presence calls for the *adoration* of the "Host," as the consecrated elements, in either kind, are called. Consistency requires that divine honor shall be paid to what is believed to be a true and actual Divinity. Hence, whenever the "Host" is presented before the people, they must kneel to it, as to a veritable God. Hence, also, those who would receive the "wafer," must receive it on bended knees.

Still further, the divine power, which is said to reside in this perpetual sacrifice by the priests at the communion altar, is extended to the world of spirits, and thus is evolved the doctrine of masses for the repose of the souls of the deceased.

By this rapid, though somewhat detailed, sketch of the historical development of the practices and doctrines of the Papal Church concerning the blessed sacrament of our Lord's Supper, it will be readily perceived that this whole fabric of errors is made finally to rest for its support upon the idea, that this ordinance is a *veritable sacrifice*, a continually repeated offering of the body and blood of Christ. If, therefore, the Scriptures disprove and condemn this idea, the entire structure must fall: and that they do condemn it must be palpable to every unprejudiced reader of the New Testament. Nothing is more clearly taught therein, than that the offering of the Lord Jesus upon Calvary's summit was the ultimate fulfillment of all the typical sacrifices which had been performed since the world began—that it was the final completed sacrifice for the sins of the world, which was never again to be repeated. Indeed, any other view degrades the infinite Saviour, and makes him finite, like ourselves. If he be infinite, then his once dying is abundantly sufficient to provide an inexhaustible atonement, and there is no need of any further offering; and if a further sacrifice is requisite, it can only be because he is finite, and because the merit of his once dying is insufficient to atone for a world's guilt. But who that is a Christian would thus degrade his Saviour?

Nevertheless, we are not left solely to general teachings and inferences in this matter. The Holy Spirit has communicated definite instruction as to this very point, in order no doubt to afford specific refutation to the false doctrines which he foresaw would be promulgated concerning it; and he who penned the Epistle to the Hebrews has recorded this instruction for our benefit. In the seventh chapter he tells us that Christ "continueth ever," and "hath an unchangeable priesthood;" .... that he "needeth *not daily* .... to offer up sacrifice, first for his own sins, and then for the people's; for this he did *once* when he offered up himself."* What more positive contradiction could we desire than this, to that false theory of a continued priesthood and a continued sacrifice in the oft-repeated ceremonies of the mass?

The same declaration is repeated, and more fully drawn out, in the ninth chapter, where it is said that the Saviour "by his own blood entered in once into the holy place, having obtained eternal redemption for us."† . . . . "For Christ is not entered into the holy places made with hands, which are the figures of the true; but into heaven itself, now to appear in the presence of God for us: nor yet that he should offer himself often, as the high priest entereth into the holy place every year with the blood of others; for then must he often have suffered since the foundation of the world: but now once in the end of the world hath he appeared to put away sin by the sacrifice of himself. And as it is ap-

* Vs. 24 and 27. † Vs. 12.

pointed unto men once to die, but after this the judgment: so Christ was once offered to bear the sins of many."*

And again in the tenth chapter we find it asserted, that in the Levitical priesthood "every priest standeth daily ministering and offering oftentimes the same sacrifices, which can never take away sins: but this man, after he had offered one sacrifice for sins for ever, sat down on the right hand of God."† And in this connection, it is expressly stated that he "taketh away the first," that is, the dispensation of perpetually offered sacrifices, "that he may establish the second," to wit, the dispensation of redemption by a once offered, infinite sacrifice. We see, therefore, that this dogma, which converts the Lord's Supper into a sacrifice, requiring priests to celebrate it, is entirely opposed to the most explicit teachings of the Bible. And it is equally opposed to the design of our Lord in the

* Vs. 24–28. † Vs. 11, 12.

institution of the Supper; since, as has already been shown, it was established as a memorial festival, to commemorate his death, and by no means as a literal acting over, again and again, of the mangling and the blood-shedding on Calvary.

Thus, the doctrine of a perpetual sacrifice in the Lord's Supper, when brought to the test of revelation, is shown to be utterly false and untenable; and with it must perish all its attendant errors.

The consecrated elements are stripped of the magical inherent efficacy superstitiously attributed to them. The masses for the dead lose all their supposed virtue, and become senseless, sacrilegious ceremonies. The kneeling before the "Host," in adoration of its asserted divinity, is shown to be, not true Christian worship, but base, inexcusable idolatry. The doctrines of transubstantiation and of communion in one kind have no longer the slightest foundation on which to rest.

Before dismissing this branch of our subject, however, we must notice an argument by which, in the view of some, transubstantiation is thought to be upheld, even if all the other doctrines of this system should be overthrown. It is said that Christ declared positively concerning the bread, when he had blessed it, "This is my body;" and that, in so important a matter, we cannot depart from a strict interpretation, but must give to the words employed their precise, literal meaning. Let us assent to this for one moment, and see where it will lead us. Of course, the same literal interpretation must be carried throughout, if once assumed: and we shall then have all four of the inspired records of this event to sustain us in the belief that Christ expected his disciples literally to drink the *cup* which he had handed them;—not what was in the cup, but the cup itself, for no mention is made of its contents. Still further, Matthew and Mark tell us that he asserted this *cup* to be his blood; while Luke and Paul agree in ascribing to him the declaration, "This *cup* is the *new testament* in my blood."

Nor can we stop here. The same literal interpretation must be carried into other recorded teachings of the Saviour. Consistency will require that, when he announces himself to the Jews as the *bread* of life, we shall consider him as at that time possessed of a body which was literally bread; and when he speaks of giving them water to drink which shall be in them a *well* of water, we shall with the same rigid strictness imagine a literal well-spring formed within each one who received from him the living water; and when he said to Simon, "Thou art a *rock*," we shall regard that disciple as actually transmuted into veritable stone.

But we pause. The illustration has been pushed thus far only to show the utter absurdity of adopting such a method of argumentation to sustain a doctrine. All languages, and especially the Oriental language in which Christ spoke, abound in such figurative modes of speech, which to literalize would be to destroy or to convert into very nonsense. It cannot for one moment be supposed, when Christ presented to his disciples the bread broken into small fragments; and when, sitting there among them as yet uncrucified, and his body still remaining whole, he spake concerning that bread, "This is my body, which is broken for you," that they would understand him to mean that he was then literally serving them with his own flesh. None who ate that bread could, by a possibility, have supposed that they were (in the very act of eating it) mangling the body of their divine Lord before his crucifixion. Nor can any of us believe it. Nor did Paul believe it, to whom the Lord Jesus himself subsequently communicated a faithful history of the whole institution of the sacrament: for, speaking of the elements after they have been consecrated, he does not call them flesh and blood, but designates them still by the same names as before the consecration, saying, "As often as ye eat this *bread*, and drink this *cup*, ye do show the Lord's death till he come."* Observe also the expression, "Ye do *show* the Lord's death"—not, ye do sacrifice your Lord afresh. Clearly, to his mind this was a representative, and not a sacrificial, ordinance.

We pass now to notice briefly *who are proper persons to participate* in this ordinance. And here at the outset we must bear in mind that there is a radical difference in the symbolical import of the two ordinances of baptism and the Lord's Supper. The receiving of baptism symbolizes what is *to be done to the subject of it* by the Holy Spirit, to wit, the washing of regeneration, and hence may be denominated

* 1 Cor. xi. 26.

the *passive* ordinance. The eating of the Lord's Supper is the symbol of that which the partaker of it is *to do himself*, that is, to feed upon Christ spiritually, to obtain from him by faith an aliment for the nourishing of the soul, and hence it may properly be designated the *active* ordinance. Baptism may, therefore, with propriety be administered to infants on the faith of their parents, as representing the purification which these parents believe necessary to be wrought upon their hearts by the agency of the Holy Spirit. But the Lord's Supper ought to be partaken of only by adults, as denoting their own intelligent desire and purpose to feed upon Christ by faith.

Moreover, unbaptized persons are not legitimately entitled to partake of the Lord's Supper, which is an ordinance designed for those who are members of Christ's visible Church on earth, having already been inducted into this visible Church by baptism.

And again, *only those who actually and*

truly believe on the Lord Jesus for the saving of their souls should draw nigh to eat at his table. Such true believers only can derive spiritual advantage from this feast. None others can appropriate to themselves that spiritual nourishment and joy which the bread and the wine symbolize. But if no benefit accrue to the participant in this ordinance, the fact of his participation will be harmful to him. No one can go away from the Lord's table in precisely the same condition spiritually as that in which he came to it. *Some positive effect* will always be produced upon every communicant. And that effect will be for good or for ill according to the state of heart with which he approaches the table.

St. Paul says, "Whosoever shall eat this bread and drink this cup of the Lord unworthily, shall be guilty of the body and blood of the Lord. But let a man examine himself, and so let him eat of that bread, and drink of that cup. For he that eateth and drinketh unworthily, eateth and drinketh damnation [that is, judgment, or condemnation] to himself, not discerning the Lord's body."* The Corinthians, to whom this admonition was addressed, had been guilty of approaching the table of the Lord irreverently, and with a profane thoughtlessness in regard to the solemn significance of the symbols employed. They had partaken of the ordinance as they would partake of any common meal, to satisfy their bodily hunger. They had so degraded it as to make it the occasion of excessive feasting, even to drunkenness. They had cherished also unholy rivalries and jealousies, had shown respect of persons, and had contemptuously treated the poorer brethren at the communion table. For all this they had suffered the severe judgments of the Lord. Many of them had become "weak and sickly," and many had already died. Yet they did not seem to know or

* 1 Cor. xi. 27-29.

to realize why these calamities had come upon them. But Paul points them to the irreverent manner in which they had celebrated the Lord's Supper as the direct cause of their sufferings. Bodily diseases and death had been sent as God's judgments against them for thus unworthily partaking of this holy ordinance of his Church. He so punished them because they had been "guilty of the body and blood of the Lord"—that is, guilty of a gross offence against the "body and blood of the Lord," by trifling with the sacred symbols which represented that body and blood.

God will ever punish those who eat unworthily—not those who feel themselves unworthy to eat, for we are all unworthy, and those who feel their unworthiness most may be the best prepared and the most welcome guests—but those who eat *unworthily*—in a thoughtless, vain, trifling, irreverent, or profane manner. Such persons eat and drink judgment, or condemnation, to themselves, "not discerning the Lord's body." Perhaps they may not now be punished with bodily diseases and premature temporal death from this cause, as were the Corinthians; but in some way they shall be made to feel God's displeasure, either in wholesome chastisement which shall lead them to repentance, or in fiercer judgments which shall work their ruin.

On the other hand, those who *worthily* partake receive great spiritual benefit. They experience the truth of that declaration of Christ, "My flesh is meat indeed, and my blood is drink indeed."* For, while they partake physically of the simple emblems of this supper, their souls do indeed derive nutriment from a spiritual contemplation of the mangled body and the poured-out blood which these emblems represent. There is, as we have seen, no inherent efficacy whatever in the emblems

* John vi. 55.

themselves; but there is verily a life-giving power in the divine atoning sacrifice which they commemorate, and they are God's appointed sign and seal of this life-giving power. They are the visible channel by which an invisible grace is communicated to such as believingly and worthily partake.

Christ's death on the cross for sinners is a holy mystery—a mystery the most wonderful and profound which has ever been brought to our knowledge as having occurred in the universe. It possesses a greater potency for good to those who are enabled rightly to discern it, and to keep it always in their remembrance, than any and all other events combined. It is no light thing, then, to come around the table of our once dead, but now risen and ascended, Lord, and to commune together upon the emblems of his passion—emblems in themselves exceedingly simple, yet vividly representing that awful, that sublime mystery—emblems instituted by himself just previous to his crucifixion.

In proportion as we are enabled, whenever we assemble at the communion table of our Lord, to make that crucifixion scene a present reality, to bring before our minds the actual event as if now transpiring, shall we be affected and profited by it. On such occasions, if we shall really, with the eye of faith, behold the Saviour hanging upon that fatal wood in agony and blood, our hearts cannot fail to be melted at such an amazing exhibition of God's compassionate regard for our race.

If, when we eat the broken bread, it brings before us that body pierced and lacerated, and makes us sensible of its vitalizing power, our souls shall indeed feed upon it, and we shall thereby derive spiritual strength.

If, when we drink the poured-out wine, it shows to us the blood streaming from those wounds inflicted upon the Lamb of

God, and impresses us anew with the life-giving energy of that blood, our souls shall quaff at the fountain, and our fainting spirits shall be revived.

God grant unto us, whenever we approach his table, such a proper and soul-profiting discernment of the body and blood of our crucified Lord!

THE END.

www.ingramcontent.com/pod-product-compliance
Lightning Source LLC
Chambersburg PA
CBHW022112160426
43197CB00009B/992